WILDLIFE OF
ROUSAY, EGILSAY
AND WYRE

WILDLIFE OF ROUSAY, EGILSAY AND WYRE

Craig Whyte

BRINNOVEN

First published in 2004 by
Brinnoven
9 Thomson Green
Livingston
West Lothian
EH54 8TA

www.brinnoven.co.uk

ISBN 1 899851 05 4

British Library Cataloguing-in-Publication Data
A catalogue record for this book is available
from the British Library

Typeset in Berthold Garamond by Brinnoven, Livingston
Printed and bound by Creative Print and Design, Wales

Contents

Foreword

That was then . . .

A cold north wind tore across the landscape. Streaks of hail raked the distant hillside. The grey pebble-dashed cottage cut a forlorn profile against a still greyer sky on the far side of what seemed like a vast, exposed field. Yet that cottage was be my refuge, and more, my home for the next four and a half months.

Four and a half months. It seemed like a grim prospect on that raw April day back in 1991. I was to be the RSPB's seasonal warden that year – the new 'birdie man' – and I was about take up my summer residence.

I reached the cottage at last, shirt pasted to my back by a cool seepage of melted hail, bulging rucksack straining at hunched shoulders. The air inside the house was cold and moist. The sofa smelt of wet dust with a hint of fungus, and the carpet looked like the bedraggled victim of a stampede . . . and this was to be my refuge.

The grey cottage was never a palace, inside or out, but gentle spring breezes blew sweet north Atlantic breaths through stagnant spaces. A lick or two of paint, applied on warm, fresh August days to walls within, helped capture the northern sunlight. And the view from the dining room table provided daily nourishment to the soul. With each breakfast I saw the shades of blue and green and, yes, of grey, redefined. Every morning was a celebration of the hues of land, sky and sea – a subtly different tricolour for each new day. Variety was the norm.

Months before, I had phoned Eric Meek, RSPB Conservation Officer for Orkney, and asked him: 'So what does the job on Rousay involve?'

'Well,' he said, 'there'll be some bird survey work, some guiding of visitors, maybe a little practical work on the reserve.' Then a pause. 'Do you play football?'

'Yes,' I answered tentatively, 'I *have* played.'

'Well,' said Eric, 'there's a game on Rousay every Sunday evening.'

And so I surveyed the hen harriers, the waders, the birds of the wood. I guided visitors on the heather-clad hills and took them to see puffins on the western cliffs. I banged in some new white-topped fence posts to mark the nature trail on the reserve. And each Sunday evening, with the sun edging towards its resting place in the north-west, I played footie with the good folks of Rousay.

I was supposed to stay for four and half months. In the end I stayed for a year and a month.

That was twelve years ago, and in the two or three years that followed, I researched and drafted this book. Then life took over, and the project was suspended in a heap of dusty documents and a couple of floppy disks. Now, thankfully, I have been given this opportunity to finally draw my project to its conclusion. But on the eve of publication, I wanted to return once more to see if anything had changed.

. . . and this is now

It was 11 March 2003, and the sun shone with more than a hint of warmth. It was good to be back, and it did not seem like eleven years and eleven months had passed since that chill April day when first I had set foot on the island.

I headed for Trumland Wood. It is choked now by the salmonberry, but snowdrops and the soft yellow buds of daffodils indicated the seepage of spring sun to the ground layer. A woodcock sprang from vegetation to my left and shot out of the wood towards Taversoe Tuick Cairn. Woodpigeons flapped noisily from the adjacent field, as my salmonberry-hindered approach warned them of human intrusion. I emerged on the hillside and, after pausing briefly to take in the expansive view of Wyre, of cone-shaped Gairsay and the table that is Shapinsay, set my sights on the Hass of Trumland. The Hass is a broad dale of heather moor and rushy grassland and in 1991 had been the breeding place of hen harrier. Sadly, hen harriers have fared less well in recent years, and there has been no nest here or elsewhere on the island for several years.

As I neared the Hass, a flurry of activity broke out; lapwings called as they tumbled from the sky, curlews sprang up to compete with them, not wishing to be left out of the spring song. They settled again quickly and the whispering breeze was the only sound once more. I trudged on through the heather, listening to the dress rehearsals of skylark song above, finding myself at last on the shoulder of Blotchnie

Fiold. My efforts were rewarded with a stunning view across the entire central moorland of Rousay, a seemingly wild landscape. The big lochs – Muckle Water and Peerie Water – lay to the west like sheets of aluminium, encompassed by the horseshoe of high ground. I surveyed the chain of hills that shelters the central moor, starting in the north-east – Kierfea Hill, great shepherd of the farming district of Sourin, watching over the green patchwork of farmland – then Twelve Hours Tower – the hill loch of Loomachun – and in the west, Ward Hill. Through a gap in the hills, I could just see the white tumult of the tidal race around the 'hallowed isle' of Eynhallow to the south-west of Rousay.

Then I heard a familiar sound – the mournful call of the golden plover, already high on the hill, just in the same spot as the pair that bred there back in 1991. I joined the nature trail then, following the post-marked route to the neighbouring summit of Knitchen Hill. A raven croaked above to show that the hill was part of his patch – one of the first birds of the year to stake a territorial claim.

I dropped down then towards the Loch of Knitchen. The red-throated divers had not yet taken up residence otherwise I would have steered clear. All the time, fulmars were peeling off the hillside, swooping down from future nest site on the rocky 'hammars' (outcrops), and gliding past with an inquisitive eye, wing tips almost shearing the tops off the heather. I returned to the Hass, over the style that marks the RSPB reserve boundary. As I did, a woodcock exploded from the foot of a Fuschia bush and darted its way down towards Trumland Wood. I guessed it to be the same bird as I had disturbed earlier, probably wondering where it was going to find peace that day.

In the afternoon I headed west. Parking by the ruined houses at Grain I followed the Quandale Dyke towards the maritime heath. All was peaceful on that March afternoon – hard to imagine that in a matter of weeks the this entire side of the island would be occupied by close to a hundred pairs of the dashing Arctic skuas, squabbling noisily over an invisible mosaic of breeding territories. I wondered where those birds were at that moment – still scattered across west African seas, perhaps – and I wondered if they were feeling the lure of this cool windswept place. I took a short rest, hunkering down behind the long wall.

It was as I stood up that I was reminded of the fickleness of the north Atlantic climate at this time of the year. I saw my fine, fresh spring day about to flee in the face of a menacing mass of grey that was about to engulf the entire west coast. I reached for my waterproofs, just in time, for in mere moments I was being lashed by a shallow-angled rain. The wind too had turned nasty and was apparently trying to rip off the waterproofs that I had just donned – my trouser legs flapped with the intensity of a drum roll and loose chin strips slapped my cheeks painfully. I continued regardless and reached the clifftop in spite of the squall. Fountains of rain and sea spray surged upwards from the cliff faces before spewing landward in a salty shower. Easy to see then why the strip of vegetation nearest the cliff was distinctly maritime in its composition, the little ginger mounds of last year's growth of sea pinks absorbing the deluge. The sea at the foot of the cliffs seethed in a white froth. In contrast, the cliffs were black now, where in the summer they are dotted white with thousands of seabirds and streaked with guano. On the stack Lobust, three early kittiwakes awaited the hordes of their kind, camped out in inclement conditions like eager shoppers the night before the January sales. Rock pipits flirted dangerously with the wind that whipped around the craggy clifftops, and a lonesome turnstone struggled to keep a foothold on a flagstone platform. Rabbits dashed headlong towards the precipice and the grey beyond, presumably turning sharply at the last moment into clifftop refuges rather than plummeting into oblivion as they appeared to be doing.

With some relief I turned inland – just as a flock of oystercatchers took to the sky – and headed into the valley of Quandale. I paused to look at the tumbling walls of the old croft houses, which the inhabitants were forced to leave behind in the nineteenth century, and imagined how different this place must have looked then. The in-bye land around those buildings is still green, favoured grazing for the rabbits and sheep that replaced the people, but elsewhere, immediately outwith the stone walls of the in-bye, the brown of heather is dominant – a striking contrast.

As I headed up the hill, back to my car, the near-gale pushing me along, a row of fulmars watched from one of the crumbling walls. I remembered that on calm days in the past I had watched them struggle to become airborne from these low-lying locations, but today, one of them, tiring of watching me, launched itself and was immediately lifted upwards on the wind, vanishing into the grey.

It was early days, not yet spring equinox. Yet in spite of the downpour I had been given more than a hint of the season that lay ahead – long summer days, daylight aplenty (payback for the winter gloom) and the almost relentless activity of breeding birds. I could hear the echoes of their song in my head, memories of my first Rousay season nearly twelve years before, and the promise of what lay just around the corner.

Acknowledgements

I would like to thank the following:

Eric Meek, RSPB Conservation Officer, Orkney (and other members of staff) and Andy Dorin, previously SNH Area Manager, Orkney, for their comments on drafts of this publication; Eric Shortland and Carol Rae, Trumland Farm, for their support and friendship during my year on Rousay.

Artwork by Bridget Woodford, Wyre.

Map by Chris and Mary Soames, previously of Rousay.

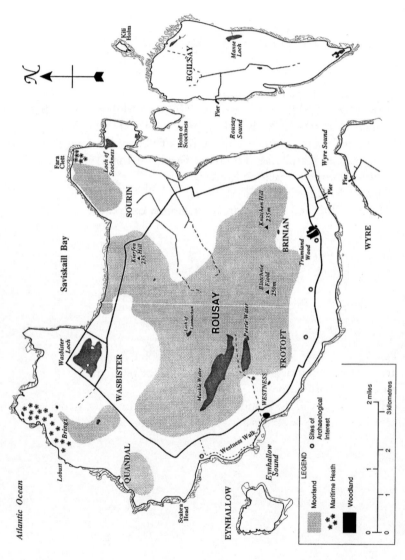

Map of Rousay, including Egilsay and the northern tip of Wyre. (Chris Soames)

Atlantic Ocean

EGILSAY

Kili Holm

Manse Loch

Pier

Rousay Sound

Holm of Scockness

Fara Cutt

Loch of Scockness

SOURIN

Saviskaill Bay

Kierfea Hill 235m

Knitchen Hill 235m

BRINIAN

Wyre Sound

Pier

Pier

WYRE

Trumland Wood

Blotchnie Field 250m

Loch of Lamlanchum

Washister Loch

ROUSAY

Peerie Water

Muckla Water

WASBISTER

FROTOFT

WESTNESS

Brings

QUANDAL

Lobust

Westness Walk

Eynhallow Sound

Scabra Head

EYNHALLOW

LEGEND

○ Sites of Archaeological Interest

Moorland

Maritime Heath

Woodland

0   1   2 miles
0   1   2   3 kilometres

Introduction
Orkney in Miniature

Orkney is a land of natural and archaeological treasures. It is a land where people and wildlife have survived side by side for thousands of years. Here, the curlew trills its spring song above ancient standing stones and the fulmar soars silently over crumbling coastal brochs. On these emerald isles of the north, lapwings, oystercatchers and gulls follow the plough across fertile fields while seabirds and porpoises cruise alongside ferries and fishing boats, watched from a rocky coast by grey and common seals.

Nowhere is the unique historical and natural heritage of Orkney more evident than on the alluring isles of Rousay, Egilsay, Wyre and Eynhallow. These jewels of the northern sea are studded with archaeological wonders – the Stone Age settlement of Rinyo; the chambered cairns of Midhowe, Blackhammar and Taversoe Tuick, which date from around 3500 BC; the Iron Age broch guarding the strait of Eynhallow Sound; the round-towered Norse church on Egilsay; the castle of the legendary giant, Cubbie Roo, on Wyre – all are tangible reminders of successive waves of immigration to this remote northern outpost.

But the legacy of the islands' peoples is not confined to the remains of their flagstone dwellings and cairns. The landscape itself is a living monument to the lives of generations of Orkney farming folk. From the maritime heath on the windswept west of Rousay to the lush fields on sheltered Egilsay and Wyre, a tapestry of wildlife habitats has been woven by islander farmers past and present, and by the sheep and cattle which they introduced. All that remains now of a scrub woodland of birch, aspen and hazel which the earliest settlers would have found are a few scattered patches of willow scrub. Instead, the Rousay hills are dominated by a large tract of heather moorland, haunt of the hen harrier, short-eared owl and golden plover, while in the lowlands, green grasslands are interspersed with lochans, colourful marshland and lowland heath or 'breck'.

The maritime heaths of the northern and western parts of Rousay epitomise the wild beauty of these north Atlantic isles. They are the summer residence of the Arctic skuas and bonxies, and home to the rare Scottish primrose. It appears to be just the way nature intended – untamed, untouched. But the maritime heath, like other habitats on the island, is the product of an alliance between nature and people, for it is not only the soil and exposed location of the heath but also moderate grazing by livestock which has shaped its unique floral structure and composition.

Only the old red sandstone cliffs on the west and north of Rousay probably remain much as they were when the first settlers set foot on the island. Even so, the seabirds which nest here on apparently inaccessible ledges have not escaped human exploitation, as the bones of shag and guillemot found in Midhowe Cairn testify. Thousands of guillemots, shags, kittiwakes, together with tysties, puffins and other seabirds still return year after year, as they have done for centuries, through Stone Age, Iron Age, Pictish and Viking eras.

With nature and history in such abundance, the compact island cluster of Rousay, Egilsay, Wyre and Eynhallow encapsulates the magical heritage of the Orkney Isles. It could readily be described as 'Orkney in miniature'. Much could be written here of the history of these islands and the people who have lived there, but here we shall concentrate on their wildlife, in particular their birds.

The central moorland of Rousay. A kestrel hovers in the westerly breeze above the slopes of the Rousay hills, alert to the sight or sound of an Orkney vole. The kestrel shares its moorland hunting ground and its mammalian prey with the hen harrier and short-eared owl.

The Central Moorland

The hilly hinterland of Rousay, encircled by the island's main road, is covered for the most part by heather moorland. The moor is little used by the island's human population and is penetrated only by a few rough tracks leading to traditional peat workings and the larger moorland lochs. It is left largely to the birds.

The moor is dominated by broad swathes of heather, a shrub that grows thickly in many places, providing cover for most of the birds in this treeless environment, as well as food in the case of red grouse. A few other dwarf shrubs resist the heather stranglehold, notably crowberry, bell heather and, locally, alpine bearberry. Attractive flowering herbs are also found. Chief among these is the common tormentil with its tiny four-petalled yellow flowers, a widespread infiltrator of heath and hill. Far less common is the serrated wintergreen which, in fact, is an Orkney rarity and was found on Rousay for the first time as recently as 1963. A variety of grasses, ferns, mosses and lichens provide further botanical interest.

This shrub-dominated flora is extensive, covering most of the hill, but locally other communities prevail, adding to the diversity of the moorland landscape. On some exposed ridges and hilltops for example, boggy pools and bare stony ground are interspersed with plant communities in which bog cotton, heath rush and mosses, particularly *Rhacomitrium,* feature strongly and the role of heather is diminished. On fine days throughout spring and summer, the clear hilltop air is filled with the twittering song of the skylark, a cheerful accompaniment to a moorland walk.

Some of the wetter areas on the hill are graced in late summer by the richly yellow spikes of bog asphodel. In other parts, wet flushes on the hillside have a profusion of tall rushes, favourite nesting places of the hen harrier, while in some drier areas woodrushes flourish. On sheltered slopes above Muckle Water and on Knitchen Hill there are patches of grass and mosses with primroses which bring a dab of colour to the moor in spring. Even more striking are the bright

Stonechat. Small, slightly plump, with an amiable demeanour, the stonechat is a bird of tall heathland vegetation. Typically, it will find the highest twig or other perch from which to utter its abrupt chinking call. The males are predominantly black with a chestnut breast and patches of white on the neck, wings and rump. They readily advertise themselves through their frequent flicking of wings and tail and their generally upright posture. Look out for it especially where there are patches of gorse.

yellow flowers of gorse which grows along the south-east fringe of Trumland Reserve. Stonechats nest among the dense spines of these bushes; blackbirds and linnets are seen here too. Elsewhere, patches of willow have emerged as on the banks of Muckle Water, attracting reed buntings to the moorland.

The heart of the central moorland is occupied by an extensive area of blanket peat and is known locally as the 'Goukheads'. Here, an association of heather, bog cotton and other heathland plants contrive to form large tussocks of vegetation, which make for difficult walking. In summer the fluffy white heads of bog cotton are a prominent feature of this inland area. However, you will have to look harder to find the diminutive insectivorous sundew, or the white flowers of the rare and beautiful round-leaved wintergreen. The latter grows only in a few favoured locations on and around the Goukheads.

During the breeding season the Goukheads plays host to a busy mixed colony of herring gulls and lesser black-backed gulls and is one of the main sites in Orkney for the latter. Other gulls nest in the surrounding hills, where their mainly white plumage is conspicuous against the heather background. The most widespread species is the great black-backed gull, which breeds both in colonies and in isolated pairs scattered across the moor. Other moorland-nesting seabirds are the skuas, the great and the Arctic, which breed here in a few isolated pairs, remote from the coastal heaths where most breeding skuas are found.

The hills of Rousay are noticeably terraced in parts and have many rocky outcrops, particularly on outward-facing slopes. The outcrops, known locally as 'hammars', are colonised by an interesting range of ferns and provide a foot-hold for another Orkney rarity, alpine saw-wort. These miniature inland cliffs are also important bird habitats, being colonised by large numbers of fulmars, and providing nest sites for the odd pair of ravens, hooded crows or kestrels.

On a largely treeless island kestrels and crows, along with woodpigeons and starlings, often nest on the ground among heather. They have been able to do this here and elsewhere on Orkney because of the lack of ground predators such as foxes, stoats and weasels, which raid bird nests in other parts of the country. On Rousay the only threat of this kind is posed by the occasional otter, brown rat or feral cat – animals more often associated with other habitats.

The central moorland of Rousay does have its share of bird predators however, notably the hen harrier and the merlin. These two raptors rate highly in Rousay's impressive list of ornithological attractions. A hunting merlin is always an exciting sight as it dashes low over the heather in pursuit of a meadow pipit, skylark or other small bird, but it is perhaps the hen harrier which impresses the most. Until recently, Rousay, together with the nearby West Mainland moors, were considered to be one of the most important centres for the species in Britain. In 1977 the number of nests on Rousay reached double figures representing around 2 to 4 per cent of the national

Hen harrier. Master of its moorland domain, the hen harrier's springtime aerial antics are among the highlights of the ornithological year. The spectacular 'skydancing' display, the mid-air passage of food from male to female, or merely a glimpse of a bird hunting low across the heather – all are dramatic and enthralling sights. Rousay is traditionally a stronghold of the hen harrier, its abundance of Orkney voles and small birds helping to sustain the island's breeding population.

total of breeding females, but the population has suffered a marked decline in recent years and at the time of publication there has not been a nest on Rousay for several years. However, a new initiative led by RSPB seeks to reverse the decline.

Hen harriers on Orkney are polygynous and the males, which are less numerous in the population, can mate with several females.

Like the merlin, the hen harrier hunts for small moorland birds, but Orkney voles are a major part of the diet too. These small, herbivorous

Twite. These busy wee finches, with their brown, streaky plumage, generally breed on the moorland, but at other times of the year their twittering flocks may be encountered around the coast, in fields or on the wires of fences. This is one of those birds, like the curlew and kittiwake, whose name is derived from its call, although the nasal twanging sound has been written variously as 'TWEit', 'twa-it' and 'chweet'. The males have a pink rump, but you are lucky if the birds stay still long enough to allow appreciation of the finer points of their plumage.

mammals are probably even more important for two other moorland hunters, the kestrel and the short-eared owl, and may account for over 80 per cent of the prey items in the owl's diet. Although primarily birds of moorland, short-eared owls have extensive ranges and are often seen hunting for voles and other small mammals close to the road and island homes.

The central moorland has a healthy population of waders during the breeding season. In spring the hills echo to the trill of the curlew, while on the moorland edge oystercatcher and lapwing perform backing vocals. Wet areas of the moorland are advertised by the drumming of snipe or the call of redshank, while in places with shorter vegetation where the ground is less undulating, golden plovers utter their mournful call.

Small birds abound on the moorland, and in addition to skylark and the ubiquitous meadow pipit are scattered pairs of wren, wheatear and twite. Even ducks in the form of mallard, teal and wigeon are sometimes found nesting in this rich and surprisingly varied hill ground.

The central moorland of Rousay has a relatively abundant invertebrate fauna which feeds, directly or indirectly, most of the birds that nest there. This, together with the scarcity of ground predators and the low grazing pressure, has allowed a bird community to develop which is comparable with that of the nationally important moors of the adjacent Mainland.

RSPB Trumland Reserve

Trumland Reserve occupies an area of 433 hectares in the south-east of the central moorland. Heather-clad hills, blanket bog, rocky 'hammars' and a moorland tarn called Loch of Knitchen make up this reserve on which most, if not all of Rousay's moorland-nesting birds, can be found. Hen harriers, short-eared owls and red-throated divers are seen throughout the breeding season in this microcosm of Orkney moorland.

The reserve features two marked nature trails; their combined starting point is found at the roadside a short distance up the hill beyond the bridge over Trumland Burn. From here the path heads northward towards the hills, passing Taversoe Tuick on the left hand side. Across the Hass of Trumland and onto the moor proper the two

Red-throated diver. The moorland lochans of the wild north are the breeding haunts of the rain goose, or red-throated diver. Here on Rousay nearly every hill lochan provides a pair with a summer residence. Superbly adapted to an aquatic lifestyle, with its streamlined shape and feet set far back on its body, the rain goose feeds in the seas around the islands, only coming inland where there is freshwater. Even then, its forays onto dry land are restricted to the water's edge, where it lays and incubates its two large eggs.

Short-eared owl. This is the owl of open country, of moorland and adjacent grassland, and the owl which hunts in daylight. Here (above) it sits on a fence post, its lemon-yellow eyes alert to the slightest movement in the field or roadside verge. The pale form and buoyant flight of the short-eared owl can be spotted in many parts of Rousay, be it hill or lowland. Listen, too, for the distant wing-clapping and courtship call as the male performs his high altitude display flight.

trails part company. The shorter trail maintains a low altitude on the south slope of the hills, while the longer strikes upward, past rows of inland-nesting fulmars, to the summits of Blotchnie Fiold and Knitchen Hill.

These are the two highest hills on the island, and the views from their tops are among the most spectacular in Orkney. To the south, the scene is dominated by Mainland Orkney, whose western hills are a mere stone's throw away across the narrow channel of Eynhallow

Sound. The highest of all Orkney's hills, the lofty grey humps of north Hoy, rise beyond those of the Mainland. Scanning eastward, the eye eventually falls on Kirkwall, Orkney's bustling capital, which lies approximately ten miles to the south-east across the Wide Firth. To the east and north, the northern isles of Stronsay, Eday and Westray stretch in a seemingly continuous land mass beyond which, in the far north, lies Papa Westray. On particularly clear days the dramatic form of Fair Isle, lying approximately mid-way between Orkney and Shetland, is visible on the horizon.

The descent from Knitchen Hill takes the trail-walker to the gorse-lined south-east fringe of the reserve and, ultimately, back to the island road.

Kittiwakes over Faraclett Head. The northern hills of Rousay sweep down towards a rugged and unspoilt coastline. The islands' coastal scenery is rich and varied, from the Atlantic cliffs on the west side of Rousay, where the kittiwakes and other seabirds nest, to the sandy shores on the sheltered east coast of Egilsay.

Coastal Heathland

The coastal heaths of northern and western Rousay boast some of the most spectacular wildlife and seascapes anywhere on Orkney. Quandale and the Brings together form Rousay's western frontier with the mighty Atlantic Ocean, while in the north-east of the island the rugged headland of Faraclett juts northwards towards Westray and the other northern isles.

Ocean exposure, soil type and human impacts have combined to create heathland habitats which are quite different to those of the relatively sheltered central moorland. Heather still dominates much of Quandale and Faraclett and grows well in parts of the former, but on seaward slopes and high ground its growth is stunted by strong winds blowing unchecked off the Atlantic. On the most exposed high parts of these moorlands crowberry competes for dominance with severely wind-clipped heather in a landscape which, in some respects, is reminiscent of tundra. Close to the sea the powerful winds are laden with salt, creating challenging conditions for plant life and resulting in an important, particularly northern Scottish brand of moorland.

Maritime Heath

On the Atlantic-facing coasts of Rousay the influence of salt spray carried in on the ocean wind is manifest in the composition of the plant community. Near the cliff tops in the west the maritime influence is so pervasive that in places there are pure swards of thrift which form attractive carpets of pink when in flower. Further back, cliff-top plants, especially sea plantain, glaucus sedge and carnation sedge, mingle with those of the moorland, forming a species-rich habitat called maritime heath. This is a unique type of heathland, peculiar to the north of Scotland, where it is found on exposed coasts with thin soils lying over old red sandstone.

A small area of maritime heath exists at Faraclett, but the Brings has one of the largest expanses of this habitat in Orkney. It is here that

Arctic tern in flight, with the paradoxically much rarer common tern in the foreground.
A flurry of grey and white wings and a collective screech of piercing calls: a tern
colony which has been disturbed by a potential intruder is a spectacular sight.
Always on edge, these specialists of the long-haul flight, marathon migrants,
swoop to defend their colonies with painful downward jabs from sharp red
bills. Well, they haven't flown all the way to Orkney from the southern ocean
to let someone trample their way across their breeding colony!

the very rare *Primula scotica* or Scottish primrose, one of Britain's few
endemic plant species, grows. The tiny, seemingly delicate purple and
yellow flowers of the plant belie its occupation of some of the most
exposed, wind-ravaged parts of Rousay. Closer examination of these
diminutive plants, however, reveals a robust build, well capable of
withstanding the elements. The Scottish primrose occurs in colonies
in which flowering occurs in two distinct periods, first in May and
later from July onwards. Other more conspicuous and widespread
flowers of the maritime heath include those of spring squill and grass-
of-Parnassus.

The bird community of maritime heath is dominated by spectacular
colonies of seabirds, including terns and skuas. The Arctic skua, one of
Britain's rarest seabirds, is near the southern limit of its range in north

and west Scotland, and the Brings and Quandale hold around 4 per cent of the national population. The colony here, recently numbering around 120 pairs, is spread over a distance of 4 km from Scabra Head to Sacquoy Head and extends inland beyond the maritime heath. Heath and moorland at Faraclett supports a second, smaller colony. These birds are well known for their acts of aerial piracy in which other seabirds, including terns and kittiwakes, are pursued with nimble twists and turns until they are forced to release or disgorge their catch of fish.

The Arctic skua shares the maritime heath with its larger relative, the great skua or 'bonxie', a stocky brown bird with distinctive dashes of white on the wings. There can often be several territories scattered along the coastal strip, each defended with intimidating head-on, mid-air rushes by its occupants. Although numerous on Orkney, the bonxie has a relatively small range, being found only in northern Scotland, the Faroe Islands and Iceland, typically on moors close to rocky coasts. The two skua species live in close proximity on the Brings, but they are uneasy neighbours and invasions of Arctic skua territories by the larger bird are vigorously repelled.

Arctic terns nest in more concentrated colonies which shift in location and size from year to year. There have been as many as 3,000 birds nesting at the Brings and Quandale in the past, but numbers have been much smaller in recent years. The terns flock together to defend their colony from potential intruders, which may be gulls, skuas or people!

The noisy aerial disputes of skuas, gulls and terns are often accompanied by the agitated calls of oystercatchers, another common species on maritime heath. Ringed plovers nest here too, especially close to the shore or cliff-top, where the top layers of sandstone are partially exposed or fragmented.

Quandale

South of the main area of maritime heath on the Brings lies the broad seaward-facing valley of Quandale. A relatively luxuriant growth of heather is found in parts of the dale, along with typical moorland flowers such as lousewort and heath milkwort. This is a grassy heathland in which mat-grass, Yorkshire fog, bents and fescues cover much of the ground, while flowers – tormentil, bird's foot trefoil and eyebright – provide dabs of yellow and white.

Quandale. The windswept undulating landscape of Quandale, overlooking the Atlantic Ocean, was once home to a thriving human population. Now, the tumbling walls of deserted homes provide nesting sites for the cackling fulmar, while oystercatchers lay their eggs amongst strewn fragments of building stones.

Here is a landscape linked strongly with the island's nineteenth-century history; the crumbling stone walls and regular lines etched on the land telling of a time when Quandale was the scene of a busy crofting township. The windswept dale is now deserted but for the sheep which range over this part of the island during part of the year. Birds now raise their young where crofting families once eked out a living. Oystercatchers have found nest sites around the ruined dwellings where short sheep- and rabbit-grazed green grass is strewn with fragments of building stones, and fulmars lay their eggs on top of the crumbling walls of old houses. Other fulmars occupy sites on the ground at the base of the long stone wall which divides Quandale from the Brings, while wheatears, summer visitors to the island, nest in the shelter of the wall itself.

Several other wader species nest in Quandale. Lapwings and golden plover lay their eggs among short grass and heather, while redshanks and snipe find cover in a few patches of marshy grassland, a habitat sometimes shared with black-headed gulls. Curlews are widespread in this lowland heathland as they are in the uplands, nesting among heather and longer grass. In Quandale they may have eider ducks for

Fulmar. The fulmar invasion of Rousay is almost complete. From its humble beginnings in the north-west tip of the island in 1905, the population spread during the twentieth century to occupy nest sites on sea cliffs and inland outcrops throughout the island. They have taken over the abandoned homes of the folk of Quandale; some even lay their single white egg on the ground, at the base of dry-stone walls. No doubt their ability to spit foul-smelling oil at intruders has contributed to their successful colonisation of such apparently vulnerable places.

neighbours. The seagoing eiders sometimes nest hundreds of metres from the shore – a long and hazardous trek for young ducklings making their maiden trip to the sea. On top of all this, meadow pipits and skylarks seem to be everywhere, adding further to a fascinating blend of terrestrial and marine birdlife.

With their wealth of birds, flora, history and spectacular seascapes the coastal heathlands are an essential part of the Rousay experience.

Farmland at Sourin, Rousay. A pastoral foreground of lush green contrasts sharply with the wild heather-clad hills in the background. These fields provide welcome feeding stations for migrating birds as well as supporting a range of resident and wintering species.

Farmland

Seen from the Rousay ferry, the contrast between moor and farmland on the island is striking. The wild heathery slopes of Blotchnie Fiold and Knitchen Hill are interrupted on their rush down to the sea by a bold band of fertile fields rising from the southern shoreline. This coastal strip, sandwiched between hill and waves, is the pasture on which the island's sheep and beef cattle are reared. These south-facing slopes may have been farmed since Neolithic times, some 5,500 years ago; a concentration of ancient burial cairns along this coast are the legacy of that prehistoric population. However, it is on the north of the island, in the districts of Wasbister and Sourin, that the most extensive tracts of farmland are found today. Here and on the neighbouring isles of Egilsay and Wyre livestock graze a gentle landscape of rolling meadows, interspersed with patches of rougher grazing and, especially on Egilsay, colourful marshland.

The transition from moorland to farmland on Rousay is abrupt in places, but often it is marked by bands of sheep-grazed rough pasture featuring patches of heather, rushes and clumps of tufted hair grass, a habitat relatively rich in food and shelter for birds and small mammals. The birds of prey of the moorland often patrol these zones, where waders and other small birds and colonies of common gulls may be found.

Away from the moorland edge, much of the farmland is in the form of permanent pasture – evergreen fields which offer little in the way of potential nest sites. Only a few species, notably lapwing and oystercatcher, have adapted to nesting here. However, in this patchwork landscape, areas of rough grassland, heath and marshy ground persist, offering refuge for some breeding birds.

Permanent pasture may be relatively poor breeding habitat, but the abundance of food to be had here attracts large numbers of birds to feed at all times of the year. In spring and summer, birds which breed on moorland, particularly curlews, may benefit significantly from the proximity of a relatively rich source of food. Similarly, woodpigeons

Mute swan and whooper swan. The two largest birds of these isles, the resident mute swan and its visiting relative from Iceland, the whooper swan. Both may be seen on and around the Loch of Wasbister in winter. The yellow-billed whooper swan may lack something of the supreme grace of the mute swan, but it is an impressive bird nonetheless. Its call is impressive too and has been likened to a blast on a bugle. Mute swans are indeed silent by comparison.

from woodland and rock doves from the coast feed on adjacent fields at this time.

It is outwith the breeding season that the largest concentrations of birds appear on the islands' farmland. Passage migrants, including golden plovers and fieldfares, are often present in substantial numbers in spring and autumn, and throughout the winter large flocks of lapwings, curlews, common gulls, crows and starlings are a familiar sight.

More locally, fields by the Loch of Wasbister are often grazed by visiting wigeon or whooper swans, while at Scockness, ringed plovers sometimes feed on fields just above the shoreline.

Many birds, then, benefit from the presence of farmland, but few species are dependent on it. For a few summer visitors, however, farms are the main providers of both nesting and feeding habitat. The pied wagtail and the swallow are two such birds, although the latter is uncommon on these islands, breeding only occasionally.

The most significant breeding species of agricultural land is the corncrake. It was once an abundant visitor to Orkney, but during the 1970s, 1980s and early 1990s the rasping call of the corncrake, familiar to generations of islanders, became a rare sound on Rousay,

Curlew. On still spring evenings the effervescent call of the curlew heralds the coming of long northern summer days. The curlew is at home in both upland and lowland, nesting among the heather or long grass. In such long vegetation it may be only the head that is visible, but that will be enough to identify the bird. That long curved bill is pretty distinctive, and is larger in the female. The haunts of the curlew extend to the shoreline, particularly outside the breeding season, where it is the largest of the wintering waders.

Egilsay and Wyre. Indeed, throughout its range the corncrake was experiencing serious declines.

The corncrake is a secretive bird that traditionally breeds in fields of long grass. It has suffered from the replacement of hay-making with the production of silage, which is harvested earlier in the year, thereby disrupting breeding.

An intensive conservation programme aimed at reversing the decline is now under way and early results have been variable. Egilsay, where corncrakes were absent in the early 1990s, is now partly managed as a RSPB reserve. In 1997 seven calling birds were heard on the island, but this early success has not been sustained, no corncrake being recorded on Egilsay in 2001 and 2002. Overall, however, there is cause for cautious optimism for the future of the bird throughout its former Scottish island strongholds, and it is to be hoped that the corncrake will once again become a regular feature on Egilsay, Rousay and Wyre.

RSPB Onziebust Reserve

The reserve comprises three areas of Egilsay farmland and marshland. Pasture on the reserve attracts breeding skylarks and waders such as lapwing, curlew, redshank and snipe, while areas of traditional hay meadow and corners of cow parsley and other tall vegetation are managed for corncrake. These corners have been created to provide early cover for the birds when they return to Orkney in May, and the hay meadow provides potential nesting habitat. The marshland area next to Manse Loch is further habitat for snipe and redshank, while the seabirds Arctic tern and black-headed gull nest here in colonies. Wild flowers, including orchids, ragged robin and yellow flag help to make this a rich and colourful place in spring and summer.

Loch of Wasbister. Also known as the Wester Loch, this, the larger of Rousay's two lowland lochs, nestles among gently sloping farmland in the north-west of the island. Several water birds nest here along the banks and in adjacent marshes. Winter is a particularly busy time at the Loch of Wasbister, with wildfowl visiting from Iceland and other far-flung breeding grounds.

Wetland

Rousay, Egilsay and Wyre have a fascinating array of freshwater lochs and marshes. All are unique with regard to size, shape and habitat, but each can be assigned to one of two broad categories, namely the upland or moorland lochs and tarns which are found on Rousay, and the more nutrient-rich waters which occur in low-lying farmed areas of the islands.

The moorland lochs, of which Muckle Water and Peerie Water are by far the largest, are the domain of the red-throated diver. The wailing call of these streamlined, long-necked birds is a characteristic sound of the Rousay hills and nearly all lochs and lochans usually hold at least one pair during the breeding season. The divers take up residence on the lochs in March and the young, of which there may be one or two, can remain until September. Most of the divers' food is obtained from the sea and they can be seen from almost anywhere on the islands, flying overhead, as they shuttle between feeding grounds and breeding lochs.

Divers apart, the smaller hill lochs have little bird life, although ducks such as mallard, teal and wigeon, which sometimes nest in surrounding heather have been known to visit them, often with their offspring.

The shores of Muckle Water and Peerie Water are of local ornithological interest in that they constitute one of the main breeding areas of the common sandpiper in Orkney. This small wader is often seen flying low across the water or standing on the banks of with its characteristic rocking motion. Breeding ringed plovers and oystercatchers sometimes share these shores with the sandpiper. The larger lochs are also visited during the breeding season by seabirds, including fulmars, gulls, great skuas and sometimes the odd cormorant.

The Muckle and Peerie Waters are relatively shallow lochs. The loch beds are stony and, in localised instances, 'peaty'. The lochs support a number of interesting water plants. At least three varieties of pondweed, including shining pondweed, grow here, as does quillwort, a tufted, tubular-leafed aquatic plant. Like ferns, quillwort reproduces by means of spores, which are produced at the swollen base of its quill-like leaves. The leaves resemble those of the water

Ringed plover. The clever camouflage of this busy little wader allows it to blend with a surprising variety of natural backgrounds. From the broken stony cliff tops of the west to the sand and shingle shores of the east, you are likely to hear its mellow musical call before you spot its scurrying shape. The nest is equally cryptic, a mere scrape in sand or shingle; the eggs like dainty pebbles. After breeding, ringed plovers often flock together to winter along the islands' shores.

lobelia, which often grows in similar habitats. On Rousay, the wide stony margins and relatively sheltered waters of the large moorland lochs provide an environment suitable to both species. Canadian pondweed, an introduced species, and floating bur-reed also grow in the moorland lochs.

Lochs which are situated amid farmland are generally richer in organic matter and nutrients and support a much wider range of bird life than their upland counterparts, due in part to run-off from surrounding farmland. The largest lowland loch on the islands is the Loch of Wasbister in the north-west of Rousay, which, together with the adjacent marsh, is the most diverse wetland site on the island. The marsh is dominated by yellow flag, with reed canary-grass, marsh cinquefoil, marsh marigold and water forget-me-not. The edge of the loch itself has stands of yellow flag and reed canary-grass, and common spike-rush, marsh pennywort and horsetail are also present. Five species of pondweed, as well as shoreweed, occur in open, shallow water, and the proximity of the loch to the sea is indicated by the presence of brackish water crowfoot. The loch is inhabited by brown trout and sticklebacks, and is frequented by otters.

The generally tall vegetation around the Loch of Wasbister and relatively rich feeding conditions provides ideal breeding conditions for many birds. Ducks such as mallard, teal and tufted ducks nest on the lochside along with coot, moorhen and mute swan, while reed buntings and sedge warblers breed in stands of reed canary-grass. Little grebes have also bred here recently.

A second freshwater loch with a small associated marsh dominated by yellow flag and meadowsweet is found in north-east Rousay, at Scockness. In the same area there is a tidal pool which is separated from the sea at low tide by a rocky bar. It has a sandy bottom with little vegetation, but is visited by shelduck and waders such as redshank.

The most interesting wetlands occur on the east side of Egilsay. Manse Loch is bordered to the west by a marsh which has stands of horsetail, yellow flag, meadowsweet, common reed and bog bean. The last forms a distinct zone along the water's edge, and the open water has a substantial cover of mare's-tail. The Lochs of Welland and Watten in the north-east corner of Egilsay are surrounded by areas of fen and marshy grassland. The fen has a good variety of sedges, with common sedge especially abundant, and herbs such as marsh cinquefoil and marsh willow-herb. The marshy grassland, which has tussocks of Yorkshire fog and tufted hair-grass, also features patches of meadowsweet. Common reeds grow across much of the Loch of Watten, in association with Chara species and horsetail. Between this area and Manse Loch is a marshland dominated by bog cotton and ragged robin, completing a chain of wetland habitats down the eastern side of the island.

The wetlands of Egilsay provide a diversity of breeding habitat for a wide range of birds. In addition to the ducks that breed on Rousay, the colourful shoveler, a duck which in Orkney is strongly associated with the northern isles, is seen here regularly, and the graceful pintail, one of Britain's rarest ducks, has been present during the breeding season. The marshy areas are populated by waders including redshank and snipe, and colonies of black-headed gulls and sandwich terns have bred side by side in the Manse Loch marsh. Several pairs of reed buntings and sedge warblers are associated with the east Egilsay wetlands.

Other wetland areas on the islands include the Loch of the Graand at the south end of Eigilsay and the loch at the Taing of Wyre, both of which are breeding sites of the mute swan.

Out of the breeding season the 'farmland lochs' support an even larger bird population. Numbers of mallard and tufted duck increase in autumn, and many other ducks, including wigeon, pochard, teal, and a few goldeneye overwinter there. Whooper swans from Iceland sometimes share the haunts of the resident mute swans, and herons frequent the water's edge. Other visitors to these compact wetland sites have included ducks such as scaup, waders including black-tailed godwit, and swifts attracted by insects flying above the water.

Trumland House and Wood. Trumland Wood occupies a sheltered location beneath Knitchen Hill, a short amble from the pier. It is one of the few places on the island where the songs of blackbird, robin, dunnock and song thrush, familiar to visitors from mainland Britain, can be heard.

Woodland

When the Norse settled on Rousay over a thousand years ago, they probably found remnants of a scrub woodland of willow, birch, aspen and hazel, which was once widespread on these islands. This is borne out by some of the place names on Rousay: Scockness, for example, is thought to be derived from *skogr*, a Norse word for 'woodland'. Buckley and Harvie-Brown, authors of *A Vertebrate Fauna of the Orkney Islands* (1888) claimed to have found further evidence of this natural woodland in the form of tree roots preserved in peat beneath the beach at Westness.

Now, due to the effects of human activity compounded by climatic factors, there is virtually no natural tree growth, only isolated pockets of willow scrub, and the only woods are the nineteenth-century plantations at Trumland and Westness. The plantations are dominated by sycamore, but Trumland has a scattering of other trees, including elm, ash, larch and spruce. Beneath this canopy there is a dense growth of salmonberry, a native of North America. The field layer includes pink purslane and lesser celandine.

These two woods, along with some of the island's gardens, contribute considerably to the diversity of bird life on Rousay. They provide nesting habitat for chaffinches, robins, dunnocks, blackbirds, song thrushes, willow warblers, rooks and sparrowhawks, which would otherwise be scarce or in some cases absent as breeding species here. Wrens breed at high density in Trumland Wood, and there have been breeding records of greenfinch and linnet.

As well as providing breeding habitat, the woods are magnets for spring and autumn migrants. Visitors have included lesser whitethroat, blackcap, chiffchaff, goldcrest, spotted flycatcher, golden oriole and Bonelli's warbler. Some of these migrants have held territory in Trumland Wood for a time and the spotted flycatcher has bred successfully. Even the long-tailed tit, a mainly sedentary species normally absent from Orkney, has found its way to the wood.

In winter the woods provide shelter for resident wrens, robins, blackbirds and woodpigeons, as well as crows and rooks. They have also attracted such visitors as woodcocks, long-eared owls and great spotted woodpeckers during the winter months, making them year-round havens for birds.

During the 1970s Trumland Wood, along with other Orkney woodlands at Binscarth by Finstown and Balfour Castle on Shapinsay, featured in a study of variations in the songs of chaffinches. Several different song types were identified, most of which occurred at all three sites. But at each woodland two songs were recorded which occurred at neither of the other locations. It has been suggested that these unique song types represent local 'dialects' of the chaffinch.

The Coast

The northern and western coasts of Rousay are rugged and beautiful. The west coast bears the brunt of the Atlantic rage, a powerful force which has carved out natural arches, blow-holes and other coastal contortions. Names such as 'Kiln of Dusty' and 'Sinians of Cutclaws' tell of a coast which has fired the imagination of those who have witnessed its splendour.

The more sheltered southern and eastern coasts are also rugged, but less grand. Here, the island's rocky palisade yields in places allowing beaches of pebbles, shingle and sand to develop. The east side of Egilsay has the most extensive sands, including a small area of dune which separates Manse Loch from the sea.

Low-lying coasts

Throughout the summer, rock pipits, oystercatchers, ringed plovers and redshanks are active along low-lying stretches of the coastline. These birds breed commonly on or close to the shore and find sustenance in the form of invertebrates among the sand, pebbles and rocks on the intertidal zone. Two colourful wildfowl species also nest on the island's coast, albeit in small numbers. These are the red-breasted merganser, which nests by the shore where vegetation affords sufficient cover, and the shelduck, found on sandier stretches of the coast on the sheltered eastern sides of Rousay and Egilsay.

Locally, Arctic terns form dense colonies on beaches of sand or shingle, where they create shallow depressions in which to lay their eggs. The Bay of Swandro on the Westness shore is one favoured site.

Around the end of May or beginning of June, female eiders lead their ducklings from nest-sites – in some cases up to a kilometre inland – to sheltered, shallow waters close to the shore. Often, broods and their mothers amalgamate to form 'creches', a strategy aimed at protecting young birds from the ever-present threat of predation by gulls or skuas.

Eider. The crooning call of the male eider, expressed with a hint of surprise in the voice, is as characteristic a sound of the sheltered coastlines as the gently lapping waves. Their sea-going congregations, or rafts, may comprise both the boldly piebald males and the dun-coloured females. The females may appear relatively drab, but that plumage provides them with excellent camouflage when they are sitting tightly on eggs among coastal vegetation in May.

Late summer and autumn sees the arrival of waders which have bred overseas and now join resident breeding species, such as oystercatcher and redshank, on the shores of the islands. Towards the end of July, large numbers of turnstones start to return to the island coasts from breeding grounds in Scandinavia, Greenland and Arctic Canada. These are followed later in the autumn by purple sandpipers, also northern breeders. Ducks, mainly wigeon, mallard and teal (species which breed in small numbers on the islands' wetlands) are part of this winter coastal community too, being found in shallow water on sheltered parts of the coast.

The cliffs

The bird community of the western and northern coasts of Rousay is quite different from that of the low shores. Here, where the coastline rises to heights of fifty metres or more, thousands of seabirds cling to

Young raven. Ravens get an early start to life; the young are often ready to take to the northern sea-wind while it still carries the icy bite of winter. Seabirds they are not, but ravens are as content to nest on the sea cliffs, above the kittiwakes and among the fulmars, as they are on the crags of the highest inland hills. The raven, when fully grown, is nearly half as large again as its relatives the rook and hooded crow. It is a characteristic bird of the wilder hills and coasts of the British Isles.

precarious, inaccessible nest sites on the ledges of Atlantic facing cliffs. The cliffs are composed of layer upon layer of flagstone, originally laid down as sediment on the bed of an extensive freshwater lake. The flagstone layers have been gnawed away over thousands of years by the pounding of ocean waves, weathering to form narrow, horizontal ledges on precipitous rock faces.

The most common species of these cliffs are the kittiwake – the gull with the strongest ties to the sea – and the guillemot, a member of the auk family. Kittiwakes occupy the narrowest ledges, where they construct nests of grassy vegetation, while guillemots cram onto broader ledges, laying a single egg on bare rock. The razorbill, a relative of the guillemot, is less common and occupies less exposed corners and crevices. Fulmars generally favour nest sites on or close to the top of the cliff.

This 'zonation' of the cliff face into different nesting habitats can clearly be seen on the sea stack known as the Lobust, which stands no more than a few metres from the mainland cliffs. The Lobust is also one of the best places at which to see two of our most attractive seabirds, the puffin and the black guillemot, both members of the auk family. Puffins nest in crevices near the top of the stack. From a certain vantage point it may even be possible to catch a glimpse of an adult puffin sitting on a nest in a dim recess in the rock. Black guillemots, or 'tysties', lay their eggs beneath boulders on the summit of the Lobust. Tysties often perch on the landward edge of this natural platform, like sentinels of the rock, proud of their smart black and white uniforms and rich red legs and gape.

Herring gulls complete the Lobust assemblage, a small colony occupying the exposed top of the stack.

Other birds which nest on the cliffs are shags, ravens, hooded crows, jackdaws, starlings, rock pipits, rock doves and, in some years, peregrine falcons. The impressive aerial attacks by peregrine falcons on their prey are surely among the most exciting spectacles of bird life on these islands.

The Rousay cliff colonies may not be quite as grand as those at Noup Head on Westray or Marwick Head on the Orkney Mainland, but they make a notable contribution to the total numbers of seabirds breeding in Orkney, which is one of the main seabird nurseries in the temperate North Atlantic.

Long-tailed Ducks. The curious call of the long-tailed duck is one of the delights of winter on these isles. The sea around the islands are populated by a wonderful range of wildlife including these and other sea duck, divers – including occasionally the very rare white-billed diver – and in the summer time, porpoises and other cetaceans.

The Sea

The sea around Rousay, Egilsay and Wyre, and indeed around Orkney in general, is rich in marine life. High productivity of plankton results in substantial stocks of small, shoaling fish such as sand eels, which are a major part of the diet of many seabirds including terns, puffins and shags.

Many seabirds feed close to the islands where they occupy different feeding niches. The black guillemot or tystie, for example, tends to remain close to the shore, where it dives for crustaceans and small fish, while others, like the shag, may feed a few kilometres offshore. Seabirds also exploit different depths in the water column. Kittiwakes and Arctic terns are splash divers, feeding close to the surface, but guillemots and razorbills dive from the surface, pursuing small fish with strong beats of their wings, often to considerable depths.

The waters around Rousay are utilised not only by birds which nest on the island, but also by seabirds from elsewhere in Orkney. Gannets, which breed on Sule Stack, over fifty kilometres to the west, are seen frequently off the north and west coasts of Rousay, diving spectacularly for fish such as mackerel or herring, and rafts of Manx shearwaters, possibly members of the Hoy breeding population, have been reported. Cormorants from colonies in other parts of Orkney are often seen around the coasts of Rousay.

Many birds, including puffins, guillemots, skuas and terns, move away from the coastal waters of Orkney after breeding, but for others the shallow, sheltered sounds of Rousay, Wyre and Eynhallow are important wintering areas.

The eider is one common resident species, present in coastal waters throughout the year. In July and August large post-breeding flocks composed mainly of flightless males become a feature of the sounds around the islands, and as many as 1,000 eiders have been counted in the sounds in winter. Shags, tysties and red-breasted mergansers also remain here during the winter months, as do a few red-throated divers.

Common guillemot and black guillemot. Two members of the auk family with contrasting habits. While guillemot cram on to noisy breeding ledges in their thousands like fans on an old football terrace, the black guillemot or tystie nests discretely under rocks and boulders. Its call is high-pitched and much softer than the gruff-voiced guillemot. The tystie's distinct white wing patches distinguish it from its much more numerous and rowdier relative, even in winter, when both relinquish their smart summer plumage.

In late September or early October the resident birds are joined by large numbers of long-tailed ducks which have come from breeding grounds in the Arctic tundra. The curious yodelling call of this attractive sea duck drifts shoreward from the sheltered waters of Rousay and Wyre Sounds on calm winter days and nights. The Orkney population of this species has been estimated at around 6,000, roughly 30 per cent of the British total, and the sounds around Wyre form one of the most important areas.

Other winter visitors to these sheltered arms of the ocean include two other sea ducks: the velvet scoter and the common scoter. These are probably birds from Scandinavian or Arctic breeding grounds, although small numbers of common scoters also breed in Caithness, a relatively short distance away to the south on the Scottish mainland.

Great northern divers also visit from breeding grounds in Iceland or Greenland, and may share their winter haunts with a few of their smaller red-throated and black-throated cousins. There have also been a few sightings of the white-billed diver close to Rousay pier. This, the largest of the divers, breeds in the northernmost parts of Russia and is a very rare winter visitor.

Common seals below Myres, on Rousay Sound. Common seals are the most frequently seen marine mammals, allowing themselves to be watched at close quarters at many coastal locations. Larger grey seals, with their longer, more pointed noises, can also be spotted. While watching seals, keep an eye open for an otter. Although not nearly as bold as the seals, the otter is equally at home here in the sheltered coastal waters of the islands.

Mammals

Seals and otters

The shores of Rousay, Egilsay and Wyre are frequented by both the grey seal and the common seal, the two species of pinniped resident to British waters.

The grey seal is by far the larger of the two, with adult males weighing up to 300 kg, more than twice the weight of male common seals. Orkney is one of the most important areas for the grey seal in Britain, supporting around 24,000, possibly around 13 per cent of the world population. The largest group of breeding grey seals in Orkney is centred around Rousay, Wyre and the Westray Firth, where pupping and mating take place on small, uninhabited islands and other remote beaches in late September and October. At other times of the year grey seals are most likely to be seen hauled out during the moult in February or March, but small numbers may be seen at any time, sometimes in association with common seals.

The smaller common seal is, in fact, less numerous than the grey, but gives the impression of larger numbers because it is more inclined to haul out on the shores of the large, inhabited islands. They are often seen loafing in sheltered waters around much of the coast and are thought to do most of their fishing closer to the shore than greys. Furthermore, the common seal does not require the same degree of isolation for the purpose of pupping, as the young are able to take to the sea just a few hours after their birth in June. In contrast, grey seal pups remain on the shore for several weeks after their birth.

Seals are now legally protected, but in the past they were hunted for their skins, oil and meat. The legend of the seal that casts its skin to become human was widespread in Orkney, as in the Western Isles and Ireland.

Good places for seal-watching on these islands include the Westness coast, the beach at Saviskaill Bay, the north-east coast of Egilsay and the Taing of Wyre.

A mammalian head peering out of the sea close to the shore is likely to be one of the two seal species, but on these undisturbed coasts it might instead belong to the secretive otter. The otter's head is smaller and flatter on top and once it has been spotted is unlikely to remain above the surface for as long as the seal's.

The size of the otter population is hard to gauge, due to the reclusive nature of the animal. Certainly, luck or a good deal of patience is required to obtain a close view. On these islands otters are primarily creatures of the coast, where they hunt for crabs and fish among the rocks and seaweed, but on Rousay they have also been seen at the freshwater lochs. Successful breeding is known to have occurred on Rousay in recent years.

A very early reference to the otter on Rousay is to be found on the *Orkneyinga Saga,* the history of the Norse earls of Orkney. It tells how Earl Paul, in Rousay in 1136 on a visit to the chieftain Sigurd of Westness, rose early one morning to go otter-hunting with a group of men. The area in which they hunted is described in the saga as being at one end of the island, near a headland, with a great heap of stones beneath, this being known as a good place to find otters.

Despite the hunting and trapping of otters through the centuries for their fur, which was once a well-known Orkney export, the otter has survived to retain its special place in the natural history of these isles.

Whales and dolphins

In addition to the seals, the waters around Orkney are visited by a number of species of whales and dolphins. Most of these cetaceans usually remain well off-shore, but a few species venture close to the coasts of Rousay, Egilsay and Wyre.

In summer, the most frequently seen is probably the porpoise, the smallest British cetacean at around 1.5 to 2 metres in length. It often occurs in sheltered water around the islands, where it probably feeds on small shoaling fish. White-beaked, Risso's and white-sided dolphins can be seen in the waters west of Rousay mostly between August and October. A sighting of a pod of orcas (killer whales) is another exciting possibility in these waters. In June 1994, seven of these, the largest members of the dolphin family, came close to a fishing boat off the coast of Quandale. This pod included an adult male – identified by its exceptionally tall dorsal fin – and a cow with a calf.

Pilot whales are seen most frequently in Orkney waters between November and January. This small whale has a low but prominent dorsal fin, the male's having a distinctive bulbous outline. This species was long valued by Orcadians for its blubber, from which oil was produced, and on one occasion sixty whales were killed in Sourin Bay, Rousay and sold for this purpose. A decomposed whale corpse, found on the beach at Westness in January 1992, probably belonged to this species.

The large whales which cruise the waters beyond the continental shelf to the west of Orkney occasionally stray closer to the islands. Minke whales are becoming regular visitors to Orkney waters and there are records of sperm whales. In 1989 the carcass of a sperm whale measuring 18 metres in length was washed up on the beach at Quandale on the west coast of Rousay.

Land mammals

Next to the otter, the largest terrestrial mammal on the islands is the rabbit. It is particularly common on farmland and moorland edges and also occurs along cliff tops. Brown hares, introduced to both Orkney and Shetland in 1830, remained fairly numerous on Rousay after disappearing from most of the other Orkney islands, but they appear to have died out here only relatively recently for reasons which are unclear.

The hedgehog is a recent addition to the islands' fauna, having been introduced to Egilsay and Wyre, but not to Rousay, during the last half-century.

Smaller mammals found on Rousay, Egilsay and Wyre are the brown rat and house mouse and, on Rousay only, the pygmy shrew and Orkney vole.

The Orkney vole is a sub-species of a species found across continental Europe. Curiously, this type of vole is absent from the British mainland although another sub-species occurs on Guernsey. The origin of the vole on Orkney is uncertain, but it may be linked to early human migration to the islands. Certainly, voles have been part of the Orkney fauna for some time, as their remains have been found in some archaeological excavations from the lower levels at Skara Brae.

The vole is widespread on several, but not all, of the Orkney islands. Its tunnels and tracks through grass and heather can be seen throughout much of Rousay, where, as a prey species, it helps sustain the island's populations of short-eared owl and hen harrier.

Systematic List of Bird Species

The following is a list of all species of Birds recorded at least once on Rousay, Egilsay or Wyre from 1974 (when the first Orkney Bird Report was compiled) to 1994 inclusive.

In many cases reference is made to records from before 1974, most notably those of T.E. Buckley and J.A. Harvie-Brown, authors of *A Vertebrate Fauna of the Orkney Islands*, published in 1891. Buckley stayed at Westness House on Rousay for six months in 1883, and his observations provide a useful insight to possible changes in the status of some species during the last century.

Records from the intervening period are provided mainly by Lack (1942, 1943), Balfour (1968, 1972), and from before 1891 by Low (1813) and Baikie and Heddle (1848).

This information is supplemented by my own observations between April 1991 and May 1992, and those of RSPB staff and others in 1993 and 1994.

Red-throated diver

Breeds on the moorland lochs of Rousay.

In 1891, Buckley and Harvie-Brown stated that there were no authenticated breeding records of this species on Orkney outwith Hoy. However, the existence of a hill loch called Loomachun, a name derived from old Norse meaning 'diver lake', suggests that this bird was present on Rousay in Viking times.

Since 1941, when just one pair was found on the island, there has been an increase in the breeding population. In the period 1986 to 1992 between 9 and 13 pairs attempted to breed each year.

In winter, small numbers have been seen in Eynhallow Sound and on the Loch of Wasbister on Rousay.

Black-throated diver

Occasionally seen in Wyre Sound in winter.

Buckley and Harvie-Brown reported that a pair frequented Muckle and Peerie Waters in May and early June 1883, and that a few pairs were present on these lochs later that summer. However, the species has never been recorded as breeding on Orkney.

Great northern diver

Winters in the sounds around the islands. The maximum count in recent years was 100 around Wyre in March 1990.

White-billed diver

A single bird in Rousay Sound on 20 April, 1976 was the first Orkney record of this species.

In 1984 one bird appeared again in Rousay Sound in late January and stayed at least until early April, and one was present in the area of Rousay Pier during winter 1989/90.

Little grebe

The species was seen by Buckley and Harvie-Brown at the Loch of Wasbister in summer 1882 and on Egilsay in June 1888.

Since 1974, there have been sightings in at least five years:

1975: two birds on Rousay, 30 September

1977: two birds on Rousay, 27 November

1989: recorded on Wyre

1993: a pair on Egilsay, 2 June

1994: bred at the Loch of Wasbister, Rousay, where two chicks were seen being fed by adults on 8 August. A pair was also present at the Loch of Watten, Egilsay, during the breeding season.

Red-necked grebe

There have been at least two records of single birds since 1965, one off Wyre before 1974 and one in Wyre Sound on 1 March, 1975.

Slavonian grebe

Five birds were present off Egilsay for a few days in late October 1982. The species also occurred in Eynhallow Sound in 1990.

Fulmar

This seabird nests at many coastal sites and inland on rocky outcrops, ruined buildings and on the ground at the foot of dry stone walls in Quandale.

Breeding was first recorded on Rousay in 1905, but now occurs in large numbers, 1,781 apparently occupied sites being recorded on

Fulmars are snow-white blobs against the dark moorland hills of Rousay. They sit confidently on a grassy bank, a heather topped wall of peat sheltering them from behind. (*Photograph Craig Whyte.*)

Rousay in 1986. Fulmars are present around the islands throughout the year.

One bird which was marked as a nestling on Rousay in 1961 was found breeding on the island thirty-three years later.

Sooty shearwater

Autumn passage migrant. There were nine off the Rousay coast on 1 September 1986. A further sighting was recorded in 1989.

Manx shearwater

Fairly large rafts have been seen off Rousay. The origin of the birds is uncertain as breeding has never been recorded on the island. They may have been members of the Hoy breeding population, non-breeders, or even long distance commuters from the Inner Hebrides. In recent years only small numbers have been recorded in the area.

Storm petrel

The existence of a small colony on Eynhallow was first proved in July 1975. The birds are not commonly seen around the islands, but nine were observed off Sacquoy Head in north-west Rousay in August 1990.

Northern gannet

The only Orkney colony is on Sule Stack, which lies over thirty miles west of Rousay, but birds are seen regularly, fishing off the island's west and north coasts.

Cormorant

The cormorant bred on Rousay in the late nineteenth century according to Buckley and Harvie-Brown. It no longer nests on the island but still visits its lochs and shores during the breeding season.

In winter, many birds move away from Orkney but some winter in the sounds around the islands. In February 1990, seventy-four were counted around Wyre and on 30 December 1994, forty were present on the small island of Kili Holm in Rousay Sound.

Shag

Breeds on the cliffs on the west of Rousay, as it did in 1883 (Buckley and Harvie-Brown).

Orkney is important for wintering shags. Around 1,000 were seen on the north coast of Rousay in February 1977 and there were 990 in the sounds around Wyre in December 1989.

Grey heron

Passage migrants and winter visitors begin to appear on the shores of sea and lochs in July. Usually birds are seen singly, but there are also reports of larger numbers:

1976: up to 12 roosted on Holm of Scockness during the winter

1983: eight at Taing of Wyre on 3 October

1991: two adults and three juveniles by the Loch of Scockness, 31 August.

White stork

Very rare visitor to Orkney. Two birds have been seen on Rousay, one on 6 June 1972 which died the following day, the second on 14 June 1977. (Three other Orkney islands had visits in the latter year, probably by the same bird)

Mute swan

Breeds regularly on Rousay. In 1991, pairs at the Lochs of Wasbister and Scockness reared broods of two and seven respectively. Breeding has also been noted on Egilsay and Wyre in recent years.

Buckley and Harvie-Brown found mute swans at only two locations in Orkney in the late nineteenth century. One of these was the Loch of Wasbister, Rousay, where the birds were described as 'semi-domesticated'.

Whooper swan

Although described as a common visitor to Orkney, only small numbers appear to visit Rousay and Egilsay.

Baikie and Heddle, writing in 1848, state that the species was then abundant on Rousay in winter.

Pink-footed goose

Passage migrant, seven of which were seen on Rousay on 8 May 1992.

White-fronted goose

Passage migrant. Seventy were seen flying over Eynhallow Sound on 28 February 1975.

Greylag goose

Passage migrant, occasionally wintering and breeding.

A flock of thirteen wintered on Wyre in 1974. Eight birds were present on Rousay on 20 June 1986, and during May and June 1991 between two and six were seen on a number of occasions on Rousay and Egilsay, perhaps originating from a small feral flock on Shapinsay. Two pairs were recorded as breeding on Egilsay in 1994.

Barnacle goose

Passage migrant. One seen flying over Sacquoy Head on Rousay on 6 June 1991 was unusually late. In 1994 a single bird was seen on Rousay on 14 May.

Baikie and Heddle (1848) were informed that breeding had occurred on Egilsay, but this cannot be confirmed.

Brent goose

Usually a rare visitor to Orkney, but more frequent in 1994, when thirteen were present on Egilsay 27–29 October.

Shelduck

Buckley and Harvie-Brown found breeding birds on the Holm of

Loch of Wasbister – winter home to a fine array of wildlfowl – with Saviskaill Bay and the cliffs of Faraclett Head in the background. (*Photograph Craig Whyte.*)

Scockness and Kili Holm in 1883 and refer to a nest found in heather on Rousay, quite far from the sea.

In recent times a few pairs have bred on Rousay at Scockness and Westness, and on the east coast of Egilsay.

Wigeon

Breeds regularly in small numbers on Rousay, and was present on Egilsay during the breeding season in 1994.

In winter it is common around sheltered coasts and on island lochs. In autumn and winter 1991 up to 140 were seen regularly on and around the Loch of Wasbister, Rousay.

Gadwall

Scarce passage and winter visitor to Orkney. One pair was seen on Rousay on 3 May 1988.

Teal

Breeds in small numbers on Rousay and Egilsay. In June 1991 a brood of ten was seen on a small moorland loch on Rousay.

Moderate numbers winter around the coasts and on freshwater

lochs. A count of 312 on Egilsay on 30 December 1994 was the second highest for Orkney that winter.

Mallard

Small numbers breed on lowland lochs and suitable areas of moorland.

In winter fairly high numbers can be seen along the coast and on lochs.

Pintail

A pair was present on Egilsay on 19 April 1993 but was not found on a subsequent visit. However, breeding may have occurred there in 1994.

There is a winter record, that of two birds on Rousay on 4 January 1977.

Shoveler

A few are sometimes seen on Egilsay during spring and summer, as in 1982, 1984, 1987, 1991 and 1994. In 1994 eight pairs were recorded there during the breeding season.

A male and two females were present at Manse Loch, Egilsay in November 1991.

Pochard

Winter visitor to lowland lochs. It is common on Orkney as a whole but there is little information specific to Rousay, Egilsay and Wyre in the literature. During winter 1991/92 up to forty, mainly males, were present at the Lochs of Scockness and Wasbister.

In 1883, four drakes were seen at Loch of Wasbister in June and July.

Tufted duck

Buckley and Harvie-Brown saw a single male at the Loch of Wasbister in mid-June 1883, but this was five years before breeding was reported for the first time on Orkney.

It now breeds regularly at the Lochs of Wasbister and Scockness and on Egilsay and is a fairly common winter visitor to the islands' lochs.

Scaup

An irregular winter visitor, the scaup is largely restricted to the large lochs of Mainland Orkney, but there are the following reports from Rousay from the mid 1970s:

1974: single male, 11 May

1975: total of 108 on two lochs, 16 February

1976: eight on Loch of Wasbister, 14 March.

Two more recent sightings occurred in 1994, both involving single birds. The first of these was at Wasbister on 20 April, the second on Egilsay on 1 November.

Two pairs with young were said to have been present at the Loch of Scockness on 28 August 1889, although these may have arrived from breeding grounds elsewhere.

Eider

Common breeding species, abundant in the sounds in winter.

Buckley and Harvie-Brown found it breeding on Holm of Scockness and Kili Holm and described it as abundant around east Rousay in 1883. One of the largest populations on Orkney was on Eynhallow where, in 1887, 200 nests and subsequently 190 broods were counted. Here they apparently benefited from protection from collection of their eggs for food.

In the mid-1970s Eynhallow's population was again estimated at around 200 breeding pairs and the population on Rousay was thought to be on the increase.

In 1991 four nests were found on moorland at Quandale and groups of females with young were seen regularly on the Westness and north-east coasts of Rousay during June and July.

In winter counts of eiders in the sounds can reach four figures, the maximum being 2,193 around Wyre in February 1990. This was also the case over a century before, over 1,000 being counted in Wyre Sound at Christmas 1886.

Long-tailed duck

Common winter visitor to the sounds around the islands. The area is of great importance to this species. A survey conducted between December 1973 and March 1974 found a total Orkney population of 6,000 birds, 30 per cent of the total British population. Of these around one quarter were found in the sounds around Rousay, Egilsay and Wyre. High counts included about 1,200 between Egilsay and Wyre in spring 1986 and 1,082 around Wyre in February 1990.

Common scoter

Rare winter or passage visitor, reported from Eynhallow Sound in 1987 and 1988.

Surf scoter

Very rare. An adult male off Wyre on 29 and 30 May 1988 is the only record from these islands.

Velvet scoter

Small numbers visit the sounds regularly in winter, but can occur in most months of the year. Three recent records are of fifteen in Rousay Sound on 21 February 1987, sixteen there in November 1989 and four off Egilsay on 21 June 1994.

Goldeneye

Winter visitor. Between autumn 1991 and spring 1992 a few were seen regularly on the Rousay lochs and in sheltered coastal waters around the islands. Earlier in 1991 a single female was seen on an Egilsay loch on 16 May.

Red-breasted merganser

Resident breeding species. Small numbers were present around the coast of Rousay in summer and winter 1991, sometimes visiting the island's lowland lochs. There were two pairs on Egilsay in 1987, ninety-nine years after Buckley and Harvie-Brown had found the species nesting on that island.

Honey buzzard

Rare passage migrant. A single bird was noted on Rousay on four dates between 14 May and 22 July 1988.

Black kite

Very rare. One seen at Trumland on 15 May 1968 was only the second record for Orkney.

Marsh harrier

Rare visitor. A single bird was seen on Rousay on 13 May 1992 and another, a female, was present on 4 and 5 May 1994.

Hen harrier*

Breeds on the central moorland of Rousay. The moors of West Mainland and Rousay have been described as the national stronghold of this raptor, although the number of nests found on Rousay ranged from between ten and twelve in 1977 to just two in 1987.

Buckley and Harvie-Brown reported only one nest in 1883 and 1888, and in the earlier year the male was shot by the gamekeeper.

There is a movement away from the island after the breeding season, but there have been recent winter records from both Rousay and Egilsay.

Sparrowhawk

A pair has bred in Trumland Wood in several recent years and passage birds have been seen elsewhere. There was a sighting in Westness Garden in 1883.

Buzzard

Rare in Orkney. There have been a number of reports of single birds from Rousay: on 3 February 1984, on 15 August 1989, and one bird was present from January to April 1990. Two birds were noted on 26 January 1990.

Rough-legged buzzard

Rare visitor. The only recent record is of a spring migrant in 1989.

Buckley saw one near Westness in November 1883 and three had apparently been shot on Rousay earlier that century.

Golden eagle

Occasional visitor to Rousay. Between 1975 to 1985 inclusive it was recorded each year with the exceptions of 1978, 1980 and 1982. Most reports were of single birds, at least half of which were immature, but two were seen together in June 1976. The following year one bird was seen regularly during the first half of the year, but in mid-July it was found coated in fulmar oil, unable to fly, and later died.

Osprey

Rare passage migrant of which there are six recent records, all of single birds. These occurred on Rousay on 6 May 1986, 30 May 1988, 27 May 1992, 19 May and 2 June 1994, and on Egilsay on 15 May 1992.

Kestrel

In recent years, one pair has nested regularly on the central moorland of Rousay, either on a rocky outcrop or on the ground among heather. Sightings may occur at any time of the year on the island.

In 1984, a bird ringed as a pullus on Rousay in July was found dying near Brora, Sutherland four months later.

Red-footed falcon

A first-year male seen at Westness between 30 May and 4 June 1981 was only the fifth Orkney record.

Merlin

In recent times one pair has bred regularly on the central moorland in areas with deep heather.

In 1991 prey items brought to the five young were mainly meadow pipits, skylarks and house sparrows, the last indicating that the merlins were also hunting in areas beyond the moor.

In 1883 Buckley sometimes saw a merlin hunting in Westness Garden in the evenings and believed that several pairs nested on Rousay.

Peregrine*

Breeds occasionally at cliffs on the west and north coasts of Rousay.

A pair frequented the western cliffs in 1883 and 1888, and in 1991, over a century later, a single bird was seen on several occasions in the same area.

Red grouse

Fairly common breeding species on Rousay moorland.

According to Low (1813) these birds were found on the 'hills of Rousa' in the early nineteenth century, and Buckley and Harvie-Brown (1891) tell us that Rousay birds were said to be the 'heaviest of any part of Scotland'. In the early 1940s the red grouse was described as common on Rousay, where it was protected, but rather scarce elsewhere in Orkney.

More recently there were fourteen pairs on Trumland Reserve in 1986, but smaller numbers in subsequent years.

Outside the breeding season flocks of up to thirty have been seen on farmland on Rousay and there have been winter records from Egilsay.

Quail

Bred on Rousay in 1958. A single bird was heard at Trumland Farm in June 1990, and between mid-June and mid-August 1992 there were reports of calling birds at Trumland, Sourin and the Loch of Wasbister.

Pheasant

Around ten birds were present on Rousay in 1978. There was a large introduction in 1984 and forty birds were seen feeding in one field in December that year. The species was recorded at only two sites during the breeding seasons of 1990 and 1991, but at eight sites in 1994.

Water rail

Passage migrant and winter visitor, seen only rarely on the islands. One was noted on Rousay on 12 May 1974 and another was shot there on 17 December 1977. A single bird was seen on Egilsay on 25 July 1994 and one heard there on 29 October of the same year.

Corncrake*

Rare summer visitor. In 1982 there were five calling birds on Egilsay and four there the following year, but generally reports from Rousay, Egilsay and Wyre during the 1980s were of just one or two birds calling on each island. In 1987 a nest was found on Rousay containing eleven eggs, but none of them hatched. Only Rousay had a calling bird in 1992 and the species was apparently absent from the islands in 1993. Calling males were noted at two sites on Egilsay in 1994, two chicks being seen at one of these in July.

There are reports from the nineteenth century of birds being present on the islands in winter, including one said to have been found in a ditch in a state of torpor in 1847, but these may be unreliable.

Moorhen

Breeding has occurred on Rousay in recent years. In 1991 birds were present at the Loch of Wasbister and also on Egilsay and Wyre during the breeding season.

Buckley and Harvie-Brown saw this bird only rarely on Orkney, but found it on Egilsay in June 1888.

Coot

Breeding has occurred on Rousay and Egilsay in recent times, and was also noted in the nineteenth century. At the Loch of Wasbister a brood of three was seen in 1991 and three or four pairs were present in 1994. A number of birds were present there during winter 1991/92.

Oystercatcher

A common breeding species on heathland and coast. A complete survey of Rousay moorland in 1981 found a total of 171 pairs and in 1987 there was a total of twelve pairs at four Egilsay sites. This wader is less common in winter, but there were counts of 107 on Rousay in December 1983 and fifty-three the following month on Egilsay.

Ringed plover

Breeds around the coasts of Rousay, Egilsay and Wyre and inland on Rousay. In 1974 three pairs bred on the shores of Muckle Water and there was a total of eleven pairs on moorland and maritime heath on Rousay in 1981. In 1990 there were twenty-three territories on the coastline of Wyre.

In winter, flocks are found on sandy bays and, at high tide, on fields near the shore. Winter counts include seventy-two on Egilsay in January 1984 and ninety-seven there in December 1994.

Golden plover

Breeds on moorland but occurs in larger numbers as a passage migrant and winter visitor. In 1943 Lack described it as abundant on Rousay but found it to be less common on the other major islands of Orkney. More recently, the largest count of breeding pairs on Rousay moorland was twenty-two in 1981.

Fairly large flocks visit the islands' farmland in spring and autumn, 128 being counted in one field at Wasbister in April 1991, and some stay on to winter. Birds were seen on Wyre in winter in the late nineteenth century.

Grey plover

Passage visitor, one of which was seen on Egilsay on 21 May 1992.

Lapwing

Breeds mainly on rough pasture and some moorland areas. In 1981 seventy pairs were counted on heathland on Rousay, although this may have been exceptional. There were at least fourteen pairs on Egilsay in 1987.

Outside the breeding season large flocks feed on farmland and in January 1986 250 were counted on Rousay.

Knot

Passage migrant of which there were forty-one on Rousay on 27 July 1990.

Sanderling

Passage and winter visitor recorded on Rousay in 1989 and 1990 and on Egilsay in 1990, 1992 and 1994. Thirty birds were counted on 30 December 1994.

Purple Sandpiper

Winter visitor. A survey in 1981 found more than 200 on the shores of Egilsay, but less around Rousay. However, two years later, on 28 December, there was a total of 269 on Rousay, 110 of which were found on the shore at Westness.

Dunlin

Passage migrant and winter visitor, breeds occasionally.

Buckley and Harvie-Brown found it breeding on the Holm of Scockness, Kili Holm and Egilsay and considered it common on Wyre. During the period 1974–82, however, no breeding was reported. In 1983 three pairs were displaying on Egilsay and since then breeding has been recorded on at least two occasions on Rousay.

In 1991 small numbers were seen on Wyre and Rousay in spring and on Egilsay and Rousay in winter.

Jack snipe

Passage migrant. Single birds were recorded on three occasions on Rousay in the latter part of 1978 and once on Egilsay in January 1984.

Snipe

Breeds in wet meadows and moorland. Counts in 1994 revealed twenty breeding pairs on Egilsay and fourteen pairs on Wyre. On Rousay breeding occurs on the central moorland and at Quandale, where two pairs were counted in 1981 and eight in 1988.

The snipe is relatively common in winter and on passage; around 100 were present on Egilsay in October 1994.

Round-topped Kierfea hill dominates the farming district of Sourin. The distant call of a curlew can be heard somewhere to the left, where farmland runs into moorland. The whispering wind is the only other sound. (*Photograph Craig Whyte.*)

Woodcock

Passage migrant and winter visitor. Large numbers were reported from Rousay in October 1976 and there were forty at Trumland Wood on 27 December 1984, but generally numbers appear to be small.

Buckley and Harvie-Brown were informed that there were two nests near Trumland in 1888 and one was found on Rousay in 1923, but there have been no recent breeding records.

Black-tailed godwit

Passage migrant, of which there have been at least three reports in recent years. Three birds were seen on Rousay on 5 September 1974 and a single bird was noted there on 29 September 1986. In 1990 nine were present at the Loch of Wasbister from 28 to 30 April.

Whimbrel

Passage migrant. There have been several recent records of sightings on Rousay and Egilsay in the months May to September.

Curlew

Common breeding species, present throughout the year. Breeding occurs mainly on moorland, where 177 pairs were counted in 1981, but also on damp grassland areas.

Flocks begin to develop in June and July and are seen feeding on farmland and coastal shores throughout winter.

Spotted redshank

Rare passage migrant of which there are three records: one bird on Wyre on 21 August 1976, one on Rousay on 6 August 1986 and another there in 1990.

Redshank

Breeds in marshy grassland and moorland on Rousay. In 1981 fifteen pairs were found on the island's moorland. Wyre had fifteen pairs in 1994.

This species is common on seashores outside the breeding season.

Greenshank

Passage migrant. Four were seen on Rousay in mid-August 1989 and there was a further sighting there in 1990.

Buckley and Harvie-Brown tell us that Rousay was the only island in Orkney on which they heard this bird.

Green sandpiper

Passage migrant. Two were seen near Peerie Water in August 1985 and there was another report from Rousay the following year. The species has also been recorded on Wyre in 1992.

Common sandpiper

Breeds on the shores of Muckle and Peerie Waters. Lack (1943) reported that there were at least ten pairs around these lochs, while elsewhere on Orkney there were very few on Mainland and just three pairs on Hoy. Balfour (1968) found that the Rousay population had halved since 1943, and since 1977 only two to four pairs have returned to the lochs each year to breed.

Turnstone

Common passage migrant and winter visitor to these islands, especially Egilsay, where 318 were counted in January 1984.

Turnstones generally leave the islands in May and begin to reappear

An Artic skua chick hunkers down among the maritime heath, while its parents wheel above, keeping a watchful eye on this brown bundle of fluff. (*Photograph William Murray.*)

in late July, although a few spent summer on Egilsay in 1988. One hundred years before, Buckley and Harvie-Brown had seen some birds on that island in full summer plumage during June and July.

Arctic skua*

Common breeding summer visitor. The following table shows how the number of occupied territories on the islands has increased during the last half century:

	1941	1961	1969	1974	1982
Rousay	0	15-20	11	51	94
Egilsay	0	0	1	2	1
Wyre	0	2-3	3-4	3	3
Holm of Scockness	0	0	2	1	1
Eynhallow	0	1	10	10	19
Total	0	18-24	27-28	67	118

Between 1989 and 1991 the population at the main colony at Quandale and the Brings increased from 97 pairs to 122 pairs. Elsewhere on Rousay there is a smaller colony at Faraclett and scattered pairs on the central moorland.

Long-tailed skua

Rare passage migrant. One was seen on Egilsay on 8 September 1989 and there were five among a colony of Arctic skuas on the Brings, Rousay on 28 May 1991.

Great skua

Summer visitor, breeding of which was first recorded on Rousay in 1955. Balfour (1967) mentions that there were five or six pairs on the island, but this had risen to sixteen territories in 1982 and to thirty-one in 1992. Breeding occurs on maritime heath and the central moorland of Rousay and on Eynhallow which held three pairs in 1992.

Black-headed gull

Breeds in marshy areas in colonies and in isolated pairs. On Rousay colonies have been noted in the Quandale/Brings area and at Faraclett, and on Egilsay by Manse Loch. In 1986 and 1987 the Rousay population was estimated at a little under 300 pairs.

Common gull

Common breeding species. Colonies may be located on heather moorland, maritime heath or rough grassland. In 1981 1,500 pairs were counted on Rousay moorland.

Large mixed flocks of common and black-headed gulls were sometimes seen feeding on the central moorland during summer 1991. In winter, flocks of a few hundred are not uncommon on farmland.

Lesser Black-backed gull

Summer visitor which breeds in a mixed colony with herring gulls on the central moorland. The species was numerous on Rousay in the 1880s and in 1981 there were over 200 pairs on the island, including ten at Quandale/Brings. However, there appears to have been a decline since then and in 1991 just twenty-two birds were counted at the main colony.

Herring gull

Breeds in colonies on moorland and at coastal sites. There were 207 pairs on Rousay moorland in 1981. A colony on the top of the stack, Lobust, on the west side of Rousay was in existence in the late nineteenth century and was thriving in 1991. In that year other colonies were located at two sites on the central moorland and on the west side of Faraclett.

Iceland gull

Rare winter visitor, reported from Wyre in 1989.

Glaucus gull

Rare winter visitor, seen on Rousay in 1990.

In 1885 the gamekeeper on Rousay shot an adult on 10 October. One or two more were seen later that year.

Great black-backed gull

Common breeding resident. In 1981 there was a total of 312 pairs on Rousay moorland. The largest colonies in 1991 were in the hills in the north of Rousay and at Quandale, and isolated pairs were widespread. The uninhabited islands of Eynhallow, Kili Holm and Holm of Scockness are haunts of this species, thirty pairs being present on Kili Holm in 1994.

Kittiwake

Common breeding species on the cliffs of Rousay. Buckley and Harvie-Brown found it nesting on these cliffs in 1883. Surveys in 1986 and 1987 found more than 5,000 pairs nesting on the island.

Kittiwakes perch on overhanging ledges; their gentle clucks are just audible above the sound of the ocean swell breaking on rocks below. (*Photograph Craig Whyte.*)

In 1991, several hundred birds were seen to gather on rocks in Saviskaill Bay in early evenings before returning to the western cliffs in a steady flow around Saviskaill Head.

Sandwich tern

Breeding has occurred on Rousay, Egilsay and Wyre. There were ten to twenty pairs on Rousay in 1973 and seventy-nine nests on Wyre in 1988. In 1993 around fifteen pairs nested among black-headed gulls in the marsh by Manse Loch on Egilsay.

Common tern

There is a shortage of information with regard to this species on these isles, but breeding may occur, at least in some years. This tern apparently bred regularly on Eynhallow in the nineteenth century, but only two birds were seen there in 1992. A pair was also present on the Holm of Scockness that year. The species was recorded on Wyre in 1983 but breeding did not occur on that occasion.

Arctic tern

Common colonial breeding species on shingle beaches, short rough pasture and, especially, maritime heath.

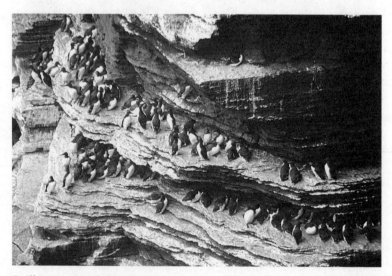

Guillemots crowd the sandstone terraces of the Lobust, while a gentle surf washes the base of the stack several metres below. (*Photograph Craig Whyte.*)

A black guillemot surveys a sunny scene of sea and cliff from a lookout post close to its nest site, hidden away in a dark rocky recess on the Lobust. (*Photograph William Murray.*)

In the early 1980s a colony at Quandale and the Brings was one of the largest in Orkney with 2,500 to 3,000 birds. In the mid to late 1980s, however, there was a sharp decline in numbers visiting Rousay and breeding success was very poor. In 1988 the 600 adults present failed to produce a single fledgling between them. There was a slight improvement in 1990 and 1991, the colony at Faraclett having the best results in the latter year.

This species is famous for its annual migration of many thousands of miles. This was demonstrated by a bird which was ringed as a pullus on Rousay in 1982 and was later recovered in Cape Province, South Africa, around 6,500 miles to the south. It can also long-lived; one bird nesting on Rousay in 1992 had been ringed as a pullus at Sandwick, Orkney twenty years before.

Guillemot

Common cliff-nesting species on the west coast of Rousay and at Faraclett. It was present at Scabra Head on the west coast in 1883. Surveys in 1986 and 1987 found more than 10,000 birds on the Rousay cliffs.

Razorbill

Common cliff-nesting species on Rousay. It was noted in the nineteenth century at Scabra Head and on the sides of the stack, Lobust, by Buckley and Harvie-Brown. Surveys of the Rousay cliffs in 1986 and 1987 found 1,014 and 676 birds respectively.

In December 1989 small numbers were recorded in Eynhallow and Rousay Sounds.

Black guillemot (tystie)

Resident in the area throughout the year, the tystie nests in crevices and under boulders and large flat stones on the coast, including the top of the stack Lobust. Eynhallow is identified as a major breeding site by Buckley and Harvie-Brown (1891) and Balfour (1973). In 1983 213 were counted there.

A few hundred birds were seen off Egilsay on 11 April 1977 and a survey of the Wyre coast in December 1989 gave a total of 169.

Puffin

Breeding pairs are scattered along the western cliffs, including Lobust and Faraclett. In 1987 118 birds were counted at these Rousay cliff sites. Eynhallow also has a regular breeding population; sixty-two birds were counted there in 1986 and 200 in 1994.

Puffin Parade. A quintet of these colourful characters of the seabird world have turned this flagstone platform on top of the Lobust into a parade ground. (*Photograph William Murray.*)

Most puffins migrate south after moulting and there is only one recent winter record, that of a single bird flying over Eynhallow Sound in December 1983.

Rock dove

Breeds on cliffs and rocky coasts. In 1994 around ten pairs also bred at the Old Manse on Rousay. Buckley and Harvie-Brown found this species in the north-west of Rousay and at Faraclett, where it is still found today. They also mention that the church tower on Egilsay was occupied.

In 1983 over 100 birds were present on Egilsay during the winter.

Woodpigeon

Breeds in woodland at Trumland and Westness and on the ground among heather. It was abundant in woodland on Rousay by the 1940s, but sixty years before Buckley had seen only two birds on the island.

Present throughout the year, woodpigeons are often seen feeding on farmland close to the woods. There were 190 birds at Trumland on 21 October 1992, that year's highest count in Orkney.

Collared dove

First reported from Rousay in autumn 1963 this bird is now recorded fairly regularly in small numbers at various times of the year.

Turtle dove

Passage migrant, recorded on Rousay in late spring 1989 and in June 1994.

Cuckoo

Regular passage migrant on Rousay. A pair was present on the island on 28 April 1988 but there has been no confirmed breeding in recent years.

Cuckoos occurred commonly on Rousay in the late nineteenth century.

Snowy owl

A single bird, probably an immature female, was present at Quandale for a few days in July 1993.

Long-eared owl

According to Balfour (1973) breeding has occurred in Trumland Wood. In recent years it has visited Rousay in winter and on spring passage. In 1976 four were present in Trumland Wood during February and March.

Short-eared owl

Three or four pairs held territory on the central moorland of Rousay each year from 1986 to 1991 and in 1994. The population in 1977 was thought to be six pairs, but nearly a century before, there had been just one nest in both 1883 and 1888.

These owls are frequently seen hunting over grassland close to roads and buildings.

Tengmalm's owl

Very rare; one was present on Egilsay on 31 May and 1 June 1986.

Swift

Passage visitor, reported from Rousay and Egilsay in recent years. There were around thirty birds at the Loch of Wasbister, Rousay on 2 August 1990.

Bee-eater

Very rare; one sighted on Rousay on 7 June 1982 was only the fifth Orkney record.

Hoopoe

The only recent record was of a bird which was caught in a byre on Rousay on 17 November 1989. It was thought to have been present on the island since the 14th, but died on the 18th. It had been ringed at Wick, Caithness earlier that month.

Wryneck

Passage migrant. Single birds have been seen on Rousay in August 1977 and on two occasions in September 1988. Buckley shot a male on the island in September 1883.

Great spotted woodpecker

Occasional visitor to Trumland Wood. A bird was seen and heard drumming there during June 1976 and the species was noted again on 17 August 1990.

Looking across nearly 5 km of wild Rousay Moorland from Blotchnie Fiold, with Muckle Water at its heart. Skylarks are singing above, and a golden plover is calling a short distance to the right. (*Photograph Craig Whyte.*)

One bird wintered on Rousay in 1968/69, staying until April. There was a sighting in Westness Garden in 1887.

Skylark

Common breeding species on grassland and moorland. There may have been an increase during the late 1980s and early 1990s. Only four pairs were counted on Trumland Reserve in 1987, but the total rose annually to over twenty pairs in 1991. There were thirty pairs on Egilsay in 1994.

Birds have been seen on both Rousay and Egilsay in winter.

Sand martin

Passage migrant. There were two on Rousay in June 1981, and some were seen at the Loch of Wasbister in 1883.

Swallow

Passage migrant and irregular breeding species. Breeding occurred on Rousay on at least one occasion in the nineteenth century and, more recently, in 1977, 1981, 1986 and 1987. In 1991 four were seen on Rousay between 10 May and 11 June, but no breeding was noted.

House martin

Passage migrant. In 1990 there was an influx to Orkney which resulted in a maximum count for Rousay of 21 on 19 May.

Richard's pipit

Rare visitor to Orkney. A single bird was seen on Egilsay on
1 November 1994.

Tree pipit

Scarce passage migrant, recorded on Rousay on 24 May 1986.

Meadow pipit

Common breeding species; there were seventy-seven pairs on Rousay's
central moorland in 1981.

Small numbers have been seen in winter on Rousay, Egilsay and
Wyre.

Rock pipit

Common resident species which breeds on rocky shores and cliff
tops. It has also nested among nettles on Egilsay and on moorland
on Rousay.

In winter it can be found inland as well as on the coast.

Grey wagtail

Passage migrant. One bird was seen on Rousay in spring 1989 and
another was present at Trumland Mill for most of September 1994.

Pied wagtail

Breeding has occurred on Rousay and Egilsay in recent years. This
species of wagtail was seen frequently around farm buildings in spring
and summer 1991.

It may have been a common passage migrant in the 1880s, as
Buckley and Harvie-Brown refer to the occurrence of great numbers
on Rousay in August and September. More recently, an influx of
twenty birds was noted on Rousay on 24 April 1994.

Seven members of the sub-species *alba*, the white wagtail, were seen
on Rousay in late August 1986.

Waxwing

Irregular passage migrant. A single bird was seen on Rousay on
18 October 1992 and there have been at least two other unconfirmed
reports in recent years. One bird was found dead on Rousay on
8 January 1974.

Wren

Common breeding resident. Up to twenty-six pairs may have nested in Trumland Wood in recent years and breeding also occurs at moorland sites. In 1883 a nest was found in an elder tree, twelve feet from the ground. Birds are also found along the courses of streams, ditches and stone walls.

Dunnock

Resident breeding species. Up to thirteen pairs have bred in Trumland Wood recently and breeding has also been recorded at Westness. Gardens and other places with bushes or small trees are frequented throughout the year.

Robin

Resident breeding species. Between 1986 and 1992 the number of pairs nesting in Trumland Wood varied from six to fourteen. Breeding was also recorded at Westness in 1990, and two singing males were present there in 1994. Robins are more widespread in winter. In 1986 forty birds were counted at Trumland, this being a relatively large spring passage.

The species was described as common and resident in 1883.

Bluethroat

Rare passage migrant. A single bird was seen on Egilsay on 3 October 1977.

Black redstart

Rare passage migrant. One was seen on Rousay on 22 April 1986.

Whinchat

Passage migrant. A singing male was heard at Quandale, Rousay in May 1985. Another male was recorded on the island in June 1994.

Stonechat

A few pairs usually breed on Rousay when the Orkney population is at a high level, usually after a run of mild winters. There were at least seven pairs on the island in 1990, and 1992 was also a good year, with four pairs present on Trumland Reserve alone.

The slopes of Quandale sweep down towards the Atlantic Ocean. Deserted nineteenth-century homesteads surrounded by grassy enclosures adorn the heather-dominated moorland. Fulmars, skuas, oystercatchers, eiders and wheatears now occupy the windswept dale. (*Photograph Craig Whyte.*)

Wheatear

Small numbers breed on Rousay. A survey of the central moorland in 1981 found a total of ten pairs nesting there and in both 1986 and 1990 two pairs were recorded on Trumland Reserve. In 1991 nesting occurred in stone walls at Quandale and Faraclett and there was one territory on Trumland Reserve.

Buckley and Harvie-Brown saw these birds feeding on the shores of Rousay, taking insects from around the seaweed.

Ring ouzel

Passage migrant, suspected of breeding in 1974 and 1977. An influx to Orkney in late October 1976 brought seven birds to Rousay, and single birds have been seen in spring in 1985, 1986, 1987 and 1989.

Blackbird

Between 1986 and 1992 the number of pairs nesting in Trumland Wood varied from four in 1987 to twenty-one in 1989. Birds have also been seen at Westness and in smaller gardens elsewhere during the breeding season, and nesting occurred on the central moorland in 1981.

The species is also a passage migrant, fifty being seen on Rousay on 22 April 1986.

Buckley and Harvie-Brown considered the blackbird to be far more common in winter, but there was little evidence of this in 1991/92.

Fieldfare

Passage migrant and winter visitor. A large passage of 300 birds occurred on Rousay in late October 1989, but normally numbers are much lower.

Song thrush

Up to seven pairs have occupied territories in Trumland Wood since 1986, a year in which breeding was also noted on Trumland Reserve. In 1992 breeding also occurred in Westness and other gardens in addition to Trumland Wood.

A passage of eighty birds occurred on Rousay on 22 April 1986.

The song thrush is apparently uncommon in winter, but was present on Egilsay in January 1982.

Redwing

Passage migrant, numbers of which vary greatly from year to year. There were 600 on Rousay in late October 1989, but only a few birds in spring and autumn 1991.

Two sources report breeding on Rousay in 1863.

Mistle thrush

Passage migrant in small numbers, recorded on Rousay in April in both 1986 and 1987.

Breeding was reported from Westness on two occasions in the mid-nineteenth century.

Sedge warbler

Small numbers breed on Rousay and Egilsay. According to Buckley and Harvie-Brown three pairs bred at Westness in 1883. In 1982 successful breeding occurred at the Loch of Wasbister and singing males have been seen at this site and another in Sourin subsequently. On Egilsay, five territorial males were present in 1990, and the following year there were singing males at Manse Loch and the Loch of Welland.

Lesser whitethroat

Passage migrant, which may have attempted to breed. In 1977 one bird sang in Trumland Wood throughout June, and in 1986 a male held territory in the wood for a few days at the end of May. Single birds have been reported in autumn in 1981 and 1989.

Whitethroat

Passage migrant, recorded in spring 1985 and in 1986, when there were two birds on Rousay on 16 June. One was singing on Rousay on 22 June 1994.

Garden warbler

Passage migrant. In Trumland Wood singing and alarm calls were heard in June and early July 1976, but breeding was not confirmed. A single bird was noted on Rousay on 3 November the same year. In 1994 a male sang in Trumland Wood on 10 June.

Blackcap*

A male held territory in Trumland Wood from 24 May to 4 June 1986.

In 1994 a singing male was recorded in Trumland Wood on several dates between the end of April and beginning of June, and two females were noted on 6 May, but breeding was not confirmed.

Yellow-browed warbler

Rare passage migrant in autumn. There were three on Rousay on 26 September 1985.

Bonelli's warbler

One seen at Trumland Wood on 17 May 1993 was only the third record for Orkney.

Wood warbler

Rare passage migrant. One was heard singing on Rousay on 23 May 1990.

Chiffchaff

Passage migrant. Small numbers appear regularly in Trumland Wood between late April and early June, and there are occasional sightings elsewhere. Breeding may have occurred in 1972, 1977 and 1994.

Willow warbler

Summer visitor. Since 1986, three to five pairs have bred regularly in Trumland Wood. In 1991 there were three territories at the same locations as the previous year.

Lack reports that only one was heard at Trumland in 1943, but tells us that the species was increasing in Orkney at the time.

Goldcrest

Fairly common passage migrant in spring and autumn. In 1989 a singing male was present in Trumland Wood between 31 May and 10 June, but there has been no confirmed breeding on Rousay.

Spotted flycatcher

Passage migrant. A few birds visit Trumland Wood in June some years.

At least one pair, possibly two, bred in the wood in 1976, and the following year birds were again present during the breeding season.

Red-breasted flycatcher

Rare passage migrant in autumn. One on Rousay on 31 October 1976 was a late migrant.

Pied flycatcher

Passage migrant. Single birds have been noted on 10 June 1979 and on 12 May and 28 August 1986.

Long-tailed tit

Very rare. There were six in Trumland Wood on 28 October 1988, but this was an exceptional year for this species in Orkney. Before that year there had been only eight records for the whole county.

Golden oriole

Rare visitor for which there are at least two recent records, both from Trumland Wood. One bird was there on 27 May 1975 and another, a female, was present on 19 and 20 May 1990.

Red-backed shrike

Passage migrant. Single birds were sighted on Rousay in June 1979 and May 1994 and on Wyre in May 1988.

Jackdaw

Small numbers are seen regularly at the cliffs at Faraclett during the breeding season. According to Lack (1942) a colony of at least twenty pairs existed at the cliffs, but there were only sixteen birds there on 7 July 1986, around six during the breeding season in 1991 (when breeding was strongly suspected), and fifteen on 11 April 1992.

Outside the breeding season jackdaws are more widespread, and in December 1991 a flock of over fifty was seen with other corvids at Trumland Farm.

Rook

Breeds sometimes in rookeries at Westness and Trumland Woods. In 1975 there were fifty-two nests at Westness, but more recent counts for both woods have been considerably smaller. In 1986 twenty-four pairs attempted to nest at Westness but were deterred by a gas gun. Fourteen pairs then moved to Trumland, where breeding was successful.

There were apparently no rookeries on Rousay in the late nineteenth century.

On 7 May 1988, 300 birds roosted at Trumland, and during winter 1991/92 flocks of up to 100 were seen frequently, feeding in fields, especially around Brinyan.

Hooded crow

Widespread breeding species, present throughout the year. Nests are found at cliff sites, in old buildings or on moorland among thick heather. There were seven pairs on the central moorland in 1981.

During 1991 and 1992 congregations of hooded crows and gulls were seen at Faraclett, where they fed on shellfish waste from the island's fish factory. On 7 May 1990 ninety-two were counted at a roost in Trumland Wood.

Raven

Resident breeding species, often seen patrolling the hills and sea cliffs of Rousay. Three pairs nested on the island in 1992 and breeding has also been recorded on Eynhallow. In 1988 a pair was present on Egilsay, and a bird was found dead there. The dead bird had been ringed two years before at Deerness on Orkney Mainland.

In 1883 breeding occurred at two sites on Rousay, but the young were shot by the gamekeeper.

Starling

Resident breeding species. It nests in many places including holes in the ground, on moorland, at cliff tops and in buildings. A nest is often located in the cairn at the top of Knitchen Hill.

An albino bird which nested on Rousay in 1990 had apparently been present on the island for at least two years.

Starlings are particularly common on farmland in winter.

Rose-coloured starling

Rare visitor from south-east Europe or Asia. The following were the second and fifth records of Orkney sightings during the twentieth century:

1962: one found dead on Rousay, 1 August

1982: an adult female present on Wyre between 31 August and 7 September.

House sparrow

Common breeding resident found mainly around farms and houses. It was very numerous in Westness Garden in 1883.

Tree sparrow

Rare visitor. In 1981 two were seen regularly at Westness in mid-June, and a single bird occurred on Rousay on 12 June 1984.

Chaffinch

Breeds in Trumland Wood. It also occurs as a passage migrant and winter visitor.

Buckley and Harvie-Brown (1891) believed that the species was only resident on Rousay in winter. Lack (1943) knew of two pairs in the wood, and singing birds were heard in 1976. More recently, between 1986 to 1992, eight to eleven pairs bred at Trumland, and birds were also present at Westness during the breeding seasons of 1991 and 1992.

In January 1976, thirty to forty birds were present on Rousay and there was a count of forty, probably passage migrants, on 3 November 1987.

Brambling

Passage migrant. Up to sixteen birds were present on Rousay between mid-September and the end of October 1982.

Spring passage was noted in 1987 and 1988, twelve being counted on 22 April 1988, and a single bird was seen on 22 May 1992.

Greenfinch

Breeding has occurred in Trumland Wood on at least one occasion in recent years. That was in 1982, when a pair was seen nest building on 22 May and three young were seen flying on 18 July. A pair was present briefly in May 1983 and June 1984, and singing was heard in May and June 1985, but breeding was not confirmed on these occasions.

Greenfinches may have been more common in the past, as there were about a dozen pairs at Trumland in 1941. In 1883 there were three or four pairs at Westness and an influx to Rousay occurred in the autumn of that year.

Goldfinch

Rare visitor. There were three birds on Rousay on 24 February 1983 and single birds there on 1 May and 30 October 1989.

Siskin

Passage migrant. Numbers and dates vary considerably as the following recent records show:

1985: thirty-five at Trumland on 26 September, that year's peak autumn count for Orkney

1986: three on Rousay on 28 and 29 April, also recorded in May

1988: one to four on Rousay in late January/early February

1991: five at Trumland, 19–21 June

1992: four on Rousay on 10 May, 18 on 27 September.

In 1994 breeding may have occurred at Trumland, where a pair was present throughout May with the male singing, and a family party of eight was seen on 2 June.

Linnet

Some years a few pairs breed in Trumland Wood and its surroundings.

Linnets bred on Rousay in the 1880s and were described as common on the island by Lack (1942). Recent breeding records, however, have referred to just one or two pairs in Trumland Wood. The species was not seen or heard in the wood in 1991 but a few birds were present in the surrounding area and may have nested in gorse.

In 1986 sixty birds visited Rousay in early autumn and a flock also wintered on the island that year.

Twite

Resident breeding species and passage migrant. During the breeding season it is seen mainly on the lower parts of the moorland and adjacent rough grassland on Rousay, and has been recorded as breeding on Wyre. It was found in trees and in ivy in Westness Garden in 1883.

A flock of thirteen was seen on the north-west coast of Rousay in mid-August 1991, and in December 1989 there were seventy on Egilsay.

Redpoll

Passage migrant. Two were present on Rousay during most of May 1986 and thirty were counted on 30 December 1988.

Mealy redpoll

A single bird was seen on Rousay on 30 October 1989.

Crossbill

Irregular visitor in summer and autumn. Sightings of up to five birds were reported in September 1976 and June 1986, and an irruption of the species in 1990 brought many to Rousay. The maximum flock that year was 126, at Westness on 22 June. The following year up to ten birds were seen on a number of occasions in June and July.

Bullfinch

Uncommon visitor, seen in autumn 1988 and winter 1991/92.

Hawfinch

Rare visitor to Orkney. A female was present on Rousay on 10 and 11 May 1994.

Snow bunting

Winter visitor. There were counts of sixty in January 1981 and thirty-two in February 1992 (both on Rousay), and 200 on Egilsay in January 1984.

Reed bunting

Small numbers breed where there are patches of willow scrub, reed beds or tall rushes. There were three pairs on Trumland Reserve and scattered pairs elsewhere in 1986. In 1991 there were two or three pairs in willow on the banks of Muckle Water, one pair in the Hass of Trumland and others by small lochs on Egilsay.

Buckley saw this bird only two or three times in 1883 and sixty years later, Lack described it as local and scarce on Rousay.

*Status Updates

Since the above list was compiled there have been a number of important changes in the status of certain bird species.

Hen Harrier

At the time of publication, no nest had been recorded on Rousay for several yerars.

Peregrine

Has twice bred on Rousay's inland crags in recent years.

Corncrake

No bird was recorded on Egilsay in 2001 and 2002.

Arctic Skua

The Rousay breeding population has recently declined.

Blackcap

Breeding was strongly suspected in recent years.

New species

Pallas's warbler

Recorded on Egilsay in 2002.